THE AMERICAN FREIGHT TRAIN

JIM BOYD

MBI Publishing Company

DEDICATION

I would like to dedicate this book to editor/designer and longtime friend Mike Schafer, who finally overcame his lifelong preference for passenger trains and expressed genuine enthusiasm and interest in a project about freight trains!

Acknowledgments

The author would like to thank the following people for their contributions to this book. Special recognition must go to Jim Shaughnessy for his superb collection of early Delaware & Hudson views and for providing permission to quote from his *Delaware & Hudson* history, first published by Howell-North in 1967. Artist John Roberts was most generous in supplying a print of his "Water Train at Pigeon Key" for use here. In addition, I would like to thank my longtime friend of more than 35 years, Mike McBride, for his sidebar story, "Those Boxcar Slogans", which appears in Chapter 7, and for his assistance in writing the portion of Chapter 8 having to do with refrigerator car lines. Thanks go to the photographers who contributed photos: R. D. Acton Sr., Marc Balkin, Steve Barry, Warren Calloway, Richard J. Cook, Mike Del Vecchio, John Dziobko, Joe Greenstein, Bob Hart Sr., Herbert H. Harwood Jr., Dave Ingles, Tom Kline, John Leopard, Alex Mayes, Mike McBride, Brad McClelland, Alexander D. Mitchell IV, Russ Porter, Alvin Schultze, Don Sims, Brian Solomon, John Szwajkart, and J. J. Young Jr. Tribute must also go to the late John Krause, for his incredible coverage of the last roundup at Parlin, Colorado, on the D&RGW narrow gauge. Of course, the book could not have been done without the support of the producer of this book, Andover Junction Publications, and their crew of Steve Esposito, Tanya Anderson, and Mike Schafer.

First published in 2001 by MBI Publishing Company, 729 Prospect Avenue, PO Box 1, Osceola, WI 54020-0001 USA

© Andover Junction Publications, 2001

Photography by the author except as noted.

Editing and book design by Mike Schafer; layout by Mike Schafer and Tanya Anderson, Andover Junction Publications, Lee, Illinois, and Blairstown, New Jersey.

MBI Publishing books are also available at discounts in bulk quantity for industrial or sales-promotional use. For details, write to Special Sales Manager at Motorbooks International Wholesalers & Distributors, PO Box 1, Osceola, WI 54020-0001 USA.

Library of Congress Cataloging-in-Publication data available

ISBN 0-7603-0833-0

On the front cover: In March 1997, an eastbound Union Pacific freight snakes through the Meadow Valley Wash along the Los Angeles & Salt Lake Route in southern Nevada. This heavily graded line is a primary corridor for freight traffic. *Brian Solomon*

On the frontispiece: The serene Juniata River valley near Duncannon, Pennsylvania, has been host to one of the busiest transportation arteries in America for nearly a century and a half. All three mainline tracks of Conrail's former Pennsylvania Railroad Harrisburg–Pittsburgh "Main Line" are lined with freight trains making their way east and west in 1977.

On the title page: The grandeur of America is subtly portrayed in this view of America's bread belt at Toluca, Illinois, in the summer of 1996 as a Santa Fe stack train cruises toward California. *Mike Schafer*

On the contents page: As if acknowledging the importance of its assignment, Nickel Plate Road Berkshire No. 743 storms eastward out of Conneaut, Ohio, Buffalo-bound with an endless string of boxcar business. *Jim Shaughnessy*

On the back cover, main photo: As one of the most aggressive freight carriers in America, Conrail was actually the new kid on the block, rising from the ashes of the once-great Pennsylvania Railroad, New York Central, Erie Lackawanna, and other down-on-their-luck Northeastern U.S. railroads in 1976. In the summer of 1997, a New York-bound Conrail freight hurries past the ancient (mid-1800s) New York & Erie depot at Susquehanna, Pennsylvania. *Jim Boyd* **Inset photo:** The Richmond, Fredericksburg & Potomac Railroad was a critical link in the flow of freight and passenger rail traffic between the North and the South, relaying trains between Washington, D.C., and Richmond, Virginia. On a balmy October day in 1986, a southbound RF&P piggyback train races through Potomac Creek, Virginia, with Florida-bound traffic. *Mike Schafer*

Printed in China

Contents

Foreword

In 1964 and 1965, the weekly Friday night meeting of the Forest City Model Railroad Club in Rockford, Illinois, was for me a greatly anticipated conclusion to a week of high-school classes. Even though I never had any homework during weekday evenings, Friday evenings were my special night off, a chance to kabitz with other

Chicago & North Western's Freeport–West Chicago, Illinois, local freight heads out of Rockford on a Friday evening in the summer of 1965.

fellows who held a reverance for railroading. Oh, we did the usual—laid some track, put in some scenery, and haphazardly operated some trains—but for me the highlight of this ritualistic jam session came when fellow FCMRRC member Jim Boyd—fresh out of photography school at Milwaukee's Layton School of Art—hauled out the projector to show us railroad slides he had taken over the previous few weeks. We were mesmerized by his ability to capture the railroading scene—and some of it was right outside the door of the club, home for which was the upstairs of an old frame warehouse along Railroad Avenue and across from the Chicago & North Western's "Pumpkin Vine" branch out of West Chicago.

One early summer evening at the club in 1965, we heard, through the open windows, the daily C&NW local trudging up out of the Rock River valley on its way back to West Chicago. Jim—always with camera at the ready—bolted from the club room, down the steps, and across the street to the tracks, taking aim at the train as it waddled out of the sunset. The result of that bit of spontaneity is at left.

Since those days, Jim and I have traveled North America extensively, often together, documenting day-to-day railroading in America. Our interests within the field, though, have always been a bit polarized. My focus was the American passenger train, which is why I spent far more time photographing Illinois Central passenger trains in Rockford than the comings and goings of North Western's lowly local. Jim was always more in tune to freight trains.

That C&NW local, though, spoke of the immense role of North American railroads in general and freight trains in particular in the development of America. Without the freight train, life in this land as we now know it would not exist. Freight trains still play a key role in sustaining that life, whether it be moving food products, manufactured goods, or critical bulk commodities such as coal, lumber, and fuel.

The model railroad club disbanded a couple years after Jim recorded this scene, and the building it was in burned to the ground in the 1980s. The towering coal bins to the left of the train have been dismantled, and the Chicago & North Western Railway was merged out of existence in 1995. And what of the IC passenger trains? They, along with most of their pre-Amtrak contemporaries, have vanished, too—their importance withered by the auto, the airliner, and Americans' desperate need for convenience. But, the local train in this scene of so long ago still plies these rails. And though its locomotive now is clad in Union Pacific livery, the train's duty remains unchanged: to move freight.

—*Mike Schafer*
Lee, Illinois

6

Introduction
The Invisible Freight Train

"It's a shame how America's railroads have disappeared." That's the reaction of a typical citizen when you mention trains these days. Big city commuters ride to work on trains provided by "transit agencies," and Amtrak occasionally makes the news when it hits a turnip truck in the middle of the night in North Carolina. But otherwise, most folks never see or hear of "trains" anymore until they get stuck by one at a grade crossing.

But North America has the finest railroad system the world has ever seen and has set the universal standards for productivity, efficiency, and technology in handling freight. While TGVs sprint across France and Bullet trains zip from island to island in Japan, these superfast passenger trains are irrelevant novelties compared to a typical American 20,000-ton unit coal train out of Wyoming bound for a power plant in Texas. And the precise flittering of passenger trains in and out of London's Paddington Station are childsplay compared to two-mile-long double-stack container trains making 70 MPH along the shore of Lake Erie or snaking down the Feather River Canyon.

Passenger trains are a political convenience, while freight trains are an economic necessity. In most countries outside North America, the railways are or were government-owned, and the glamorous passenger trains are national status symbols—and generally horrific money losers. In the U.S., the local, state, and federal governments have chosen to focus transportation subsidies on automotive and air travel, from local roads and small-town airports to the Interstate highway system and O'Hare International Airport, while the rest of the world subsidizes its rail systems. This suits the geography and governmental philosophies of the countries involved. America is married to the automobile because that's what best suits the geography, economy, and temperament. Compact and densely populated island nations like England and Japan put their money into rail systems and the local mass-transit networks that support them. But in the twenty-first century, more and more of the world's nationalized railways are being privatized along the American pattern, with the passenger trains subsidized as necessary to provide the services that are considered essential.

When it comes to freight capacity, however, the world has never seen the likes of the North American system. A typical American unit coal train would crush the tracks of the famous Trans-Siberian Railroad, and an American double-stack container train could never get out of the port at Southampton, England, without destroying every overhead bridge it encountered.

Even the automobiles that Americans love so much probably have more rail mileage in their component parts than their warranties would cover on the odometer! Coal from West Virginia and ore from Minnesota were combined in Ohio to make steel that was shipped by rail to Detroit to be fabricated into unibodies that will be mated to engines built in Kansas City and shipped by rail to Michigan. Then the final new car spends four days in a trilevel freight car before being delivered to the dealer in Southern California. But the proud new owner only knows that the next time the family goes to visit grandma in Arizona, it will be by car, because "there aren't any more trains."

In this book we'll look at the rich history and technology of the American freight train. It's been an essential part of the nation's fabric and culture since the 1820s, and it has literally made possible the life we enjoy today.

Welcome aboard, for a fascinating journey where you need a waybill, not a ticket.

—Jim Boyd
Crandon Lakes, New Jersey

A Chicago-bound Chicago, Burlington & Quincy freight from St. Paul, Minnesota, evaporates into the evening at a lonely grade crossing near Shabbona, Illinois, in late winter 1970.

The early history of railroading in America is summarized in this one photo, taken in July 1980 at Lanesboro, Pennsylvania. The northbound freight is on the Delaware & Hudson, the oldest continuously operating transportation company in the country, dating back to the D&H Canal Company in 1823. Overhead is the magnificent Starrucca Viaduct, built by the six-foot-gauge New York & Erie Railroad in 1847 and kept in continuous service ever since. Starrucca is 1,200 feet long and 110 feet high with 17 stone arches. By 1980 the Erie was part of Conrail.

1

Tramways to Railroads

Stuff tends to be heavy, and it usually needs to be somewhere else to be of use to anybody. That's where the freight train comes in. It is the most cost-efficient and rapid means of overland transportation ever devised to serve the needs of man. In the earliest times, he harnessed beasts to carry his burdens and expanded his overland technology with wheeled carts and wagons. But roads were crude and rough, and movement was slow and expensive.

The first narrow-gauge railway in the world was the two-foot-gauge Ffestiniog in Wales, which used these four-wheel wagons to move slate from the quarries high above the town of Blaenau Ffestiniog 12 miles to the Cardigan Bay seaport of Porthmadog. The railway opened in 1836 and used gravity to roll the trains of cars downhill, controlled by simple hand brakes. For the return trip, horses pulled the empty cars back up to the quarries. Steam locomotives replaced the horses in 1863. After the line was shut down following World War II, it was revived in 1955 as a tourist attraction. This train of vintage slate cars, used for historic demonstrations on special occasions, was parked behind the Porthmadog engine shop in 1987.

The two-foot-gauge Ffestiniog Railway in Wales was opened in 1836 to move slate downhill to Cardigan Bay on the Irish Sea. Abandoned following World War II, it was revived as a tourist hauler in 1955 and returned to steam operation. On September 23, 1991, a double Fairlie articulated steam locomotive was dropping downhill through the picturesque community of Penrhyn with the tracks laid atop massive stone walls. The region's slate was used for roofing and building material throughout the United Kingdom, and the Ffestiniog was state-of-the-art transportation in its day.
ALEXANDER D. MITCHELL IV

Rivers and oceans provided a smooth means of transportation for boats and ships, which is why early commerce developed along the great waterways of the world. Gold and grain and salt and spices and silk and even ice moved from continent to continent in sailing ships for more than 2,000 years, but the overland treks from the sources to the seaports were often laborious.

The earliest images of wheeled vehicles on a smooth fixed guideway relate to mining and quarrying operations, where four-wheeled carts rode on wooden "rails" with the guiding flanges either on the wheels or the tracks themselves. Gravity, with the help of cables, was the usual motive power for moving the loads downhill from the dig site to the waterway below. Horses or mules or even manpower then returned the empty carts back uphill. These captive operations are generally known as "tramways."

BEGINNINGS IN GREAT BRITAIN

One of the earliest tramways, still in existence today, is the Ffestiniog Railway in North Wales. In the eighteenth century, slate was a prime building material for housing and roofing, and huge gray mountains of high-quality slate surrounded the community of Blaenau Ffestiniog. The nearest navigable waterway was at Portmadog on Cardigan Bay off the Irish Sea about 12 miles to the south, but a wagon road down the rugged hillsides

would not have been economically practical to transport the heavy and fragile slate.

As early as 1804 in Wales, a six-mile, horse-powered tramway, the Swansea & Mumbles, had been built on the south coast to haul coal from a mine to the seaport. The slate around Blaenau Ffestiniog was even more valuable, and gravity and geography worked in favor of a tramway. On May 23, 1832, King William IV signed an act of Parliament authorizing civil engineer James Spooner to survey a right-of-way that would wind down the hills from Blaenau Ffestiniog, dropping 700 feet in a little over 13 miles with a carefully calculated rate of descent of 1.1 percent (a drop of 1.1 feet every 100 feet), increasing to 1.5 percent to maintain speed where the resistance of curves would tend to slow down the rolling cars. Groups of loaded four-wheel slate cars, coupled together with chain links, would coast downgrade, with men controling their speed using simple hand-brake levers. The empty slate cars would then be pulled back up the hill behind horses.

The cars, extending barely 18 inches above the rail, were small enough to be easily pushed by one man but would carry two tons of slate. Returning uphill, one horse could pull a train of cars on the rails that would have required 40 horses on a wagon road! The economics of rail transportation were undeniable. Steam locomotives were already in use when the Ffestiniog was chartered, and Spooner envisioned such motive power from the onset, even though no machine suitable for his needs had yet been built.

The Ffestiniog was not the first railway. Railroads had gotten their start in England in the early 1820s as haulers of both passengers and goods, and the Stockton & Darlington Railway was already experimenting with steam locomotives by 1825. Four years later a competition was held at Rainhill to select the motive power for the proposed Liverpool & Manchester Railway, a competition won by George Stephenson's *Rocket*. But these were essentially flatland operations focused on replacing stagecoaches and freight wagons (in fact, the British still refer to railwaymen in stagecoach terms like "driver" and "guard," and the early locomotives had no weather protection for the crews, since stagecoach drivers, guards and footmen traditionally rode outside the carriage).

The flatland railways were being built to the "standard gauge" of 4 feet, 8½ inches between the rails (based on the width of the historic Roman chariot roads in England) that was being promoted by locomotive builders George and Robert Stephenson and often referred to as "Stephenson Gauge." The curving and hilly Ffestiniog slate railway, however, was built to the inexplicable gauge of 23½ inches for economy and ease of construction. The world's first "narrow gauge," the Ffestiniog was opened for business in 1836 and became an immediate commercial success.

Steam locomotives replaced horses for the uphill return on the Ffestiniog in 1863, and the locomotives permitted it to add passenger and general merchandise traffic to the slate haulage. This upgraded the Ffestiniog from a single-commodity tramway to a full service "common-carrier" railroad. The Ffestiniog chugged its way into the twentieth century hauling slate, merchandise,

and passengers, but following the Great Depression of the 1930s, trucks on improved highways took away much of the slate business. The railroad was shut down following World War II, but it was revived as a tourist railroad in 1955.

THE DELAWARE & HUDSON

On January 5, 1825, as the Stockton & Darlington was coming to life in England, a group of bankers and businessmen was meeting in the Tontine Coffee House at Wall and Water streets in New York City. They were being warmed by a clean, blue-flamed blaze in the fireplace. Merchants Maurice and William Wurtz of Philadelphia had brought in this load of "stone coal" from their lands east of Scranton, Pennsylvania, and they

The main map below illustrates the Delaware & Hudson Canal Company's original route between Olyphant, Pennsylvania, and Kingston, New York— a combination gravity railroad/canal transportation artery. The inset shows how the famous Erie Canal, the D&HCC, and selected future rail routes of the D&H, New York Central, Erie, and Lackawanna all related in terms of their geographic position in early Northeastern transportation. (Not all rail lines are shown, and predecessor lines are shown in some instances.)

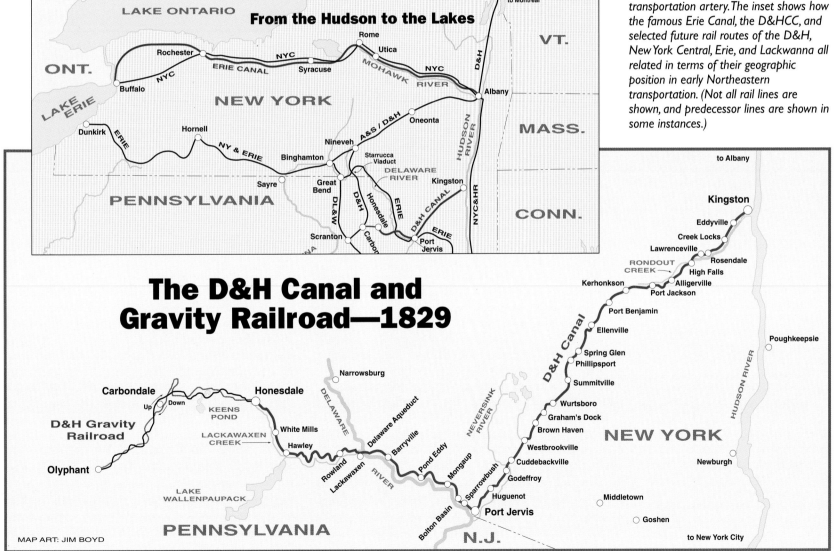

were seeking financial backing to build a combination tramway and canal to get this new home-heating fuel to the New York City market.

The city of Philadelphia was already being supplied with this anthracite coal by the Lehigh Coal & Navigation Company's mines and Schuylkill (SKOO-kuhl) Canal out of the Lehigh coalfields southwest of Scranton. The Wurtz brothers were going after the untapped New York market by climbing over the mountain ridge between their mine at Carbondale and the potentially navigable Lackawaxen Creek at Honesdale, which fed into the Delaware River. A 48-mile canal overland between the Delaware and Hudson rivers would provide an all-water route from the head of Lackawaxen Creek to New York Harbor and a ready market for their coal.

According to Jim Shaughnessy's excellent history, *Delaware & Hudson* (Howell-North, 1967), canals were already becoming a thriving business in North America, highlighted by the legendary 364-mile Erie Canal (started in 1817 and completed in 1825) linking the Hudson River at Albany with Lake Erie at Buffalo. By April 23, 1823, the Pennsylvania and New York legislatures had authorized the Wurtz brothers to build their Delaware & Hudson Canal along Lackawaxen Creek, down the Delaware River and eastward across country from Port Jervis to the Hudson River at Kingston.

A slack-water canal was built for 25 miles alongside the sometimes-turbulent Lackawaxen Creek to the town of Lackawaxen, where it crossed over the Delaware River on an aqueduct

suspension bridge engineered by John Roebling (which is intact today as a road bridge). The canal then continued down the New York side of the Delaware for 23 more miles to Port Jervis before turning inland over the flats toward Kingston and the Hudson River.

But before the anthracite coal could reach the canal basin at Honesdale on Lackawaxen Creek, it had to be hauled over the 950-foot summit of Moosic Mountain. Chief Engineer John B. Jervis designed a 17-mile railroad with steam-powered winches on inclined planes to pull the eastbound loaded coal cars up to the summit, where they would be dropped downhill by gravity. The line was built to 4-foot 3-inch gauge with strap-iron rails atop wooden stringers. There were five hoisting planes on the west slope for the upbound loads and three on the downbound east slope. The one-ton railcars could each carry 2½ tons of coal and were handled in five-car groups on the planes.

Although horses were used to pull the loaded railcars over the relatively flat stretches between the hoisting planes, Jervis had designed the railway for the use of steam locomotives, even though at that time no steam locomotive had ever operated in America. In 1828 he sent his 25-year-old assistant, Horatio Allen, to England to purchase a locomotive from George Stephenson.

In 1828, 25-year-old Horatio Allen went to England to purchase locomotives for the gravity railroad. On August 8, 1829, he took the throttle of the Stourbridge Lion at Honesdale and entered the history books with the first run of a steam locomotive in North America. Unfortunately, the Lion was too heavy for the track and never entered service.
D&H ARTWORK, JIM SHAUGHNESSY COLLECTION

Allen contracted with Stephenson for one locomotive, the *America*, similar to the soon-to-be-historic *Rocket* (which had not yet performed and gained fame at Rainhill), and three more of a different design manufactured by Foster & Rastrick of Stourbridge (the *Delaware*, the *Hudson* and the *Stourbridge Lion*). In January and May 1829, the *America* and *Lion* arrived in New York City and were steamed up for public demonstrations,

turning their wheels while mounted up on blocks but not moving on rails. Both locomotives were shipped up the Hudson River to the D&H Canal, but only the *Lion* actually arrived in Honesdale. The *America* mysteriously vanished from the history books at the Kingston canal terminal.

On August 8, 1829, Horatio Allen took the throttle of the *Stourbridge Lion* and made a historic six-mile round trip from the canal basin at

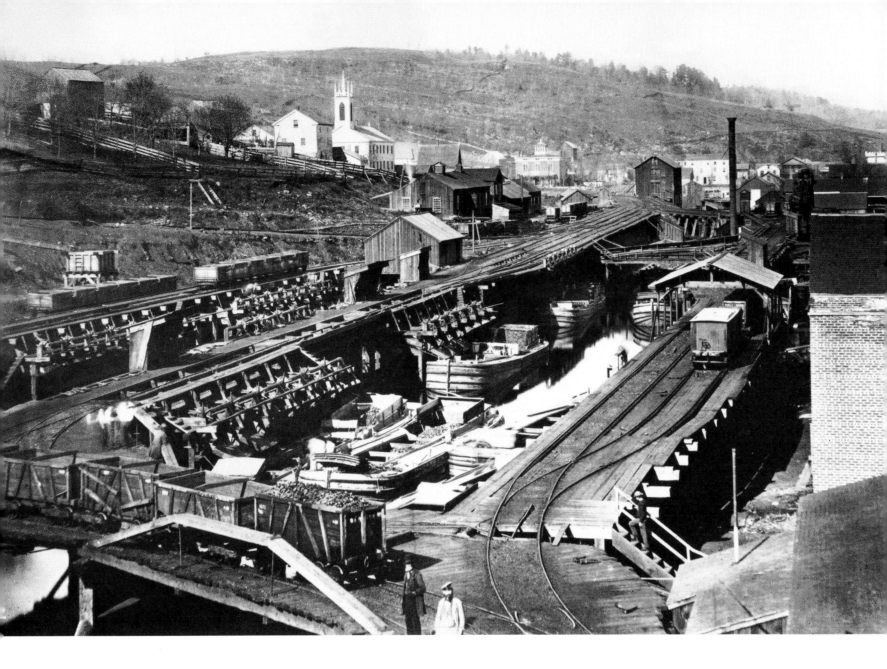

Honesdale to Seelyville and back. This was the first locomotive to run on rails in America. But after a second test run on September 9, it was obvious that the track would not support the seven-ton machine, and the *Lion* was retired to a makeshift shed without ever entering service. It was scrapped around 1870. The *Delaware* and the *Hudson* arrived in Kingston and vanished without historic record just like the *America*.

Although the 108-mile canal had been open for a year, on October 9, 1829, the first load of anthracite coal came over the gravity railroad into the basin at Honesdale. The Delaware & Hudson Canal Company was now

fully in business carrying coal from Carbondale as well as local products like cement and lumber to the eager customers in New York City. Like most canals of the era, the D&H was thus a common-carrier in that it would carry anyone's goods and passengers for a fee, rather than being captive to one company.

Over the next three decades the gravity railway and canal were operated successfully and upgraded in numerous ways. No further attempts were made to employ locomotives until 1860, when two steam engines were purchased for use on the extensions on the Carbondale end to new mines farther down the valley. By this time, steam

The upper boat basin at Honesdale circa 1860 is a fascinating study of transportation technology. The five railcars in the foreground are at the base of the final plane off the mountain. Several of the older, smaller canal boats have been "hipped" with sideboards to increase their capacity. On this site today is a museum housing a full-size replica of the Stourbridge Lion, and adjacent is the north end of the Lackawaxen & Stourbridge shortline railroad that connects with the old Erie Railroad main line at Lackawaxen, Pennsylvania. D&H, JIM SHAUGHNESSY COLLECTION

continued on page 18

The Racket Brook Breaker was alongside Plane No. 4, about halfway up the west side of the mountain above Carbondale on the alignment of the original gravity railroad. The system was improved and extended between its original construction in 1829 and the mid-1860s. Here, a crew of men is shoving empty cars into the loading shed, while a cut of loads awaits movement up the hill. Steam-powered winches were used to drive the cables that hauled the cars up the steep inclined planes. The track at far right is the "main line" uphill, while the track adjacent to it is a shorter plane that goes to a series of yard tracks that enter the far side of the breaker at the level of the horizontal bridgework visible above the loading shed. The track gauge is 4-foot 3-inches, and by the time this photo was made, the original wood-stringer and strap-iron rail had been replaced with "modern" T-rail. G.M. BEST COLLECTION, COURTESY JIM SHAUGHNESSY

After of the failure in 1929 of the *Stourbridge Lion* because it was too heavy for the track, the gravity railroad operated with cables and mule power until 1860, when it bought two 4-foot 3-inch gauge 0-4-0s from W. Cook & Co. The first of these was the Major Sykes, which was wrecked in a collision in 1871 and rebuilt in 1872, emerging as shown here as an 0-6-0. The engine remained in service on the D&H gravity railroad until it was retired in 1889. *G.M. BEST COLLECTION, COURTESY JIM SHAUGHNESSY*

Realizing that the future was in a "real" railroad rather than the canal, the D&H struck out north from Carbondale and joined with the Albany & Susquehanna to complete a six-foot-gauge main line to Albany, New York, and beyond. In this view at Nineveh, New York, in 1880, the freight train behind 2-6-0 No. 57 is en route from Oneonta to Binghamton and will get 2-6-0 No. 70 as a pusher up Belden Hill. J. J. YOUNG JR. COLLECTION, COURTESY JIM SHAUGHNESSY.

Continued from page 15

technology had made great progress, and the locomotives were virtually "off the shelf" items. The Civil War brought boom times to the D&H Canal, and the gravity railroad was hard-pressed to keep up with the shipping demands.

The D&H Canal had opened in 1828, and in 1832 the New York & Erie Railroad had been chartered to build from New York Harbor to the Delaware River and along New York's "Southern Tier" to Lake Erie at Buffalo. The six-foot-gauge railroad was completed in 1851

and would have a profound influence on the future of the canal.

Realizing the potential for year-around service provided by the railroad when the canal froze up in the winter, following the Civil War the D&H changed direction—literally—and worked with the Erie to extend its rail operations north from Carbondale to connect with the Erie main line at Lanesboro, Pennsylvania, site of the Erie's legendary 1,200-foot-long, 110-foot-high stone-arch Starrucca Viaduct. By acquiring other existing

railroads and building new lines, the D&H rapidly expanded northward. By late 1875 it had reached all the way to Montreal, Canada!

Even as its steam trains were carrying coal to Albany and Canada, the D&H's gravity railroad and canal continued to serve the New York City market. Passenger service was inaugurated on the gravity railroad in 1877 and became a popular tourist attraction, but the canal was finding it difficult to compete with the rapidly expanding rail network in the region. Both the gravity railroad and the canal were shut down in

1899, as the Delaware & Hudson continued to prosper as a railroad. Ironically, the D&H Railroad never duplicated the Honesdale-Kingston route of the D&H Canal but took off in entirely different directions.

The Delaware & Hudson, chartered on April 23, 1823, survived as an independent railroad until January 1991, when it was purchased by the Canadian Pacific Railway, and operates as part of that system to this day. For 168 years, the Delaware & Hudson was America's oldest continuously operated transportation company.

Traversing the area where it all began, a Delaware & Hudson southbound freight eases downhill at Carbondale, Pennsylvania, in the summer of 1978. By that time, very little of the anthracite mining that had prompted the creation of the gravity railroad and D&H Canal remained in the area and was generating very little rail traffic. The D&H Railroad had gone on to make its fortune on long-distance merchandise traffic.

Competition
and Cooperation

tories like that of the Delaware & Hudson were repeated all across the U.S. in the three decades between 1830 and the Civil War. Future great names like the Pennsylvania Railroad and Baltimore & Ohio were taking their first faltering steps with cantankerous teakettle locomotives and crude trackwork in the 1830s. The B&O's diminutive *Tom Thumb* locomotive became eternally famous for losing a race with a horse in 1830, and in 1831 the *Best*

INSET: One of the secrets of success of America's railroads is the Type E automatic knuckle coupler, adopted as the national standard by the Association of American Railroads in 1932, based on the Master Car Builders (MCB) coupler that was standardized in 1888. This rugged coupler, combined with George Westinghouse's air brake, permits the two-mile-long trains that we take for granted today. RICHARD J. COOK

OPPOSITE: Typical of a steam-era freight train was this Sierra Railroad scene at Sonora, California, in October 1971 of a "mixed" (freight and passenger) train powered by 2-8-0 NO. 28 (built by Baldwin of Philadelphia in 1922) out of Jamestown. Although this was a special train for photographers, it carried revenue freight and did the "real" work at the lumber mill in Standard that would otherwise have been done by a diesel-powered run that day. JIM BOYD

21

A train is much harder to stop than it is to start, and early braking systems were rather rudimentary but effective. Here in 1983, the Pennsylvania State Railroad Museum's authentic operating replica of the John Bull (built by the Pennsylvania Railroad in 1940) employs the same human-powered brakes used by the Camden & Amboy original, which dates back to 1831. The "brakeman" beneath the gigtop faces rearward and applies the brakes by pushing his feet against a long lever, which is connected to the wooden brake shoes on the wheel treads of the tender. Each car trailing the locomotive would also have a hand brake.

Friend of Charleston in South Carolina became the first locomotive in America to enter regular revenue service (and shortly thereafter blow up in a fatal boiler explosion). But the Camden & Amboy's rugged little *John Bull*, built by Stephenson in England in 1831, worked so well that 15 identical sisters were built. They powered the trains which would soon grow to become the greatest land transportation system of the steam era, the Pennsylvania Railroad.

In a fascinating look at what was being hauled by these earliest railroads, John H. White Jr., of the Smithsonian Institution, described in his authoritative book, *The American Railroad Freight Car* (Johns Hopkins University Press, 1993), the tonnage carried on the B&O in a single week in April 1832, when it extended only 13 miles between Baltimore and Ellicott's Mills, Maryland. The tally was: 1,721 barrels of flour, eight hogsheads of tobacco, 127 tons of granite, 31 tons of iron, 16 tons of lime, 36 tons of paving stone, three tons of planks, 3.5 tons of leather, 5 tons of tan bark, and 2.75 tons of horse feed (no mention was made of any of that latter going to the horse that had embarrassed the *Tom Thumb* two years earlier).

This would be the typical pattern for the developing freight railroads: building supplies, foodstuffs, and heavy raw materials.

THE IDEA OF INTERCHANGE

Most of the early railroads developed in splendid isolation and were each unique unto themselves. The Delaware & Hudson designed its own track to its own gauge (distance between railheads) of 4 feet, 3 inches, and connected a mine to a canal—Point A to Point B with just a nasty hump in between. The Camden & Amboy connected New York Harbor with the Delaware River as an overland shortcut between New York and Philadelphia that depended on waterways at either end. The C&A was heavily influenced by its locomotive builder, Stephenson of England, and adopted the Stephenson "Standard Gauge" of 4 feet, 8½ inches. Throughout the 1830s and 1840s, railroads tended to be built as portages between waterways and were engineered to local standards.

As the railroads grew in the 1840s and 1850s, trackwork and rolling stock were designed for safe and economic operation at about 10 MPH. This was much faster than canal boats or horse-drawn wagons and was considered quite competitive. Faster speeds tended to beat up the track and equipment and become much more costly overall. Ironically, it was the occasional runaway train that proved that cars could move safely at much higher speeds—until they hit a curve or obstacle and ended the discussion with a bang.

By the 1850s, many railroads were connecting end-to-end to create long-distance routes, but the idea of direct interchange of loaded cars was still alien. After all, these were potentially rival companies. It was very common for a load to be handled from one railcar to another via wagon or riverboat on a long journey. This "break-bulk" concept was the norm in water transport and seemed quite logical for railroads. Besides, the handling of goods between the carriers employed armies of laborers and provided the opportunity for their bosses to "sample" the goods that were being transferred. It was just jolly good business, and if the politicians were getting their cut, many cities passed laws forbidding direct interchange between railroads to ensure that those in power had continuing "access" to this commerce.

Adding to the situation was the variety of track gauges that were being used. There were at least a half dozen commonly used gauges between four feet and six feet. As late as 1861, the 4-foot 8½-inch standard gauge made up only a little over 50 percent of the mileage, with five-foot gauge making up another 20 percent. In addition, wheel, trackwork, brake, and coupler standards were virtually nonexistent.

Meanwhile, back in England, in 1841 the bank clearing house that handled most of the inter-railway financial transactions had begun encouraging its clients to cooperate in direct interchange of each others' freight and passenger cars. The economic advantages of moving a loaded car over a variety of railroads from origin to destination without intermediate unloading and reloading was obvious. However, it took brawling-in-the-wilderness Americans a bit longer to catch on.

In fact, it took a Civil War. Although most of the Deep South had been built to South Carolina's 5-foot gauge, Ohio's unusual 4-foot 10-inch gauge effectively broke the North's transportation system into incompatible segments to the east and west. Pittsburgh became bogged down with transfers between the Ohio lines and Eastern carriers like the standard-gauge B&O. The labor-intensive break-bulk handling that had been such great economic sport in peacetime threatened the North's very existence, with Rebel armies on the march.

All sorts of bizarre engineering schemes were tried to overcome the handicap, from the swapping of trucks (the wheelset assemblies beneath the cars) to dual-gauge track. Privately owned railcar companies even got into the business with freight cars equipped with wide-tread wheels that could roll, albeit a bit drunkenly, on both standard- and Ohio-gauge track.

In the early years, there was little or no standardization of track gauge, and direct interchange was discouraged, often by law. Here on the Delaware & Hudson at Dickson, Pennsylvania, in the early 1870s, a northbound passenger train from Scranton to Carbondale was running on the multi-gauge main line that was needed to accommodate all the equipment used in the area. The right rail is the running rail common to all gauges. At the extreme left is the 6-foot gauge rail for Erie equipment, and next to it is the 4-foot 8½-inch standard-gauge rail, while the 4-foot 3-inch gravity system rail is on the inside. G.M. BEST COLLECTION, COURTESY JIM SHAUGHNESSY

As the Delaware & Hudson was growing northward toward Albany from the Carbondale coalfields, Oneonta, New York, became an important terminal and the site of a major freight-car shop (the building in the center distance with the two round-top doors). Here in 1875, the shops were being used to convert Albany & Susquehanna equipment from 6-foot to standard gauge. In the distance are two roundhouses for the steam locomotives, as well as a large pile of cordwood for fuel. The railroad names on the boxcars in foreground include the Syracuse, Binghamton & Northern; Wabash; Erie; DL&W; and Grand Trunk.
D&H, COURTESY JIM SHAUGHNESSY

Following the war (1861–1866), the railroads began to work toward standardization to take advantage of the economic potential of interchange. In 1867, the Master Car Builder's Association was formed to develop and implement standardization for railway equipment. It adopted the 4-foot 8½-inch standard gauge for the U.S. network and soon outlined such basic standards as coupler height, wheel contours, and clearance dimensions (the maximum width and height of cars).

Before interchange of equipment could be practical on standard-gauge lines, however, there were some other technical aspects that needed to be standardized if cars were to move safely from one railroad to another. The most important of these were couplers and brakes.

THE QUESTION OF COUPLING

From the earliest tramways, railroaders had struggled with the need to join the cars and motive power together to create a train. Simple hooks and chain links were used at first, but the problem of "slack" between the cars made for a jerky and dangerous ride. Good railroad couplers would have to deal with both tension (pulling) and compression (pushing) forces.

By the Civil War, most railroads were using some form of iron "link-and-pin" couplers that utilized an oval link held by removable pins in a cast pocket. The rounded edges of the coupler pocket acted as buffers for the compression loads. The couplers were mounted onto the car's underframe with a "draft gear" equipped with heavy springs and friction plates that would hold the coupler in place but permit it to flex slightly side-to-side and up-and-down and would cushion the fore-and-aft shocks of normal operation.

Although effective and economical, link-and-pin couplers were dangerous to manipulate, since the trainman had to get between the moving cars and hold the link in position by hand to insert it

into the pocket—and then get his hand out a split second before the pockets slammed together. And, of course, there was little standardization in pocket size, link dimensions, or pin diameter from one railroad to the next.

All sorts of bizarre coupling mechanisms were tried and patented in the years before and after the Civil War, but it was a veteran Confederate Army colonel, Eli Hamilton Janney, who solved the problem with a simple but rugged mechanism that locked together like a pair of human hands. An internal pin locked the knuckles in place when the coupler was closed from the impact of bringing the cars together. A lever to the outside edge of each car made it possible to couple and uncouple from safely beside the cars.

Janney was granted a patent for his coupler in April 1873, but the industry was in no particular hurry to adopt it. In 1877 the powerful Pennsylvania Railroad agreed to test the coupler, liked what it saw, and began applying it to passenger cars.

In 1888 the Master Car Builder's Association got Janney to release the patents for his jaw contours so that other manufacturers could produce compatible couplers. This was the first step toward ultimate standardization, utilizing the Janney design as the universal "MCB coupler."

In March 1893, safety legislation was passed that gave the railroads five years to equip all rolling stock with automatic couplers. In 1932 the Association of American Railroads adopted the modern standard "Type E" coupler that could be produced by any manufacturer but would be universally interchangeable. As the needs for stronger, safer, and more specialized couplers developed following World War II, a variety of new couplers was introduced, but all remained compatible with the AAR Type E, which is still the standard today.

The most common of these specialized couplers is the "Tightlock," introduced in the early 1950s, which uses additional external jaws to more tightly grip each other and prevent vertical motion. Tightlocks will generally not come apart in a wreck and tend to minimize "scattering" of cars in a derailment. Tightlocks and safety "shelf" couplers are most commonly used on piggyback cars and tank cars to minimize hazards in a wreck.

STOP IT!

It is easier to start a train than to stop it. Freight trains have always been the heaviest things to move on land, and the physics laws of motion

and inertia are powerful factors in the handling of a train. Regardless of speed or motion, even the simplest freight car must have some sort of braking system so that it will not roll away when parked on a track somewhere.

The earliest freight cars, like the gravity cars on the Ffestiniog and D&H, were equipped with simple levers that would shove brake shoes against the treads of the wheels. This same lever system was also used on stagecoaches and horse-drawn wagons.

The earliest locomotives usually had no brakes on the driving wheels but used the wheels of the tender (the adjacent car that carried the coal and water supply) for braking. The Camden & Amboy's 1831 *John Bull* had both a hand lever on the tender and a long lever with a foot pedal that reached almost to the top of the tender's roof (see page 22). The "brakeman" would ride atop the roof and use both feet to shove out on the lever to apply the brake shoes to the wheels. The considerate C&A even included a canvas gigtop to protect him from hot cinders and the weather.

The first power braking systems were simple "steam jam" brakes which used a steam-actuated piston to apply pressure to the brake shoes on the driving wheel treads. It was controlled by a single valve in the cab.

ABOVE LEFT: One of the few railroads operating today with link-and-pin couplers is the three-foot gauge Pine Creek Railroad at Allaire State Park in New Jersey. Chris Kimler demonstrates how the link is held in the coupler casting with the removable pin. Imagine having to hold the pin like this as another coupler was being moved against the other end of the link and getting your hand out of the way before they crashed together.

ABOVE: The inherent safety of the modern AAR Type E coupler is obvious as engineer Dick Roden uses the "cut lever" from safely outside the equipment to open the front knuckle on Canadian Pacific 4-6-2 2317 at the Steamtown National Historic Site in Scranton, Pennsylvania, in September 2000. When the couplers come together, the knuckles are pushed shut, and the top pin drops into place, securing the knuckle in the closed and locked position.

The author demonstrates the operation of hand brakes on a string of D&RGW stock cars on the Durango & Silverton Narrow Gauge Railroad near Silverton, Colorado, in June 1988. Although these cars are equipped with air brakes, they retain the vertical-staff handbrakes that were the only braking system before the 1880s. Note the ladders to the roof of the cars, which were also equipped with catwalks over their tops. In the handbrake era, one brakeman would handle about five cars and carry a baseball-bat-sized wooden club to help snug the wheels. *MARC BALKIN*

The most popular handbrake system in the 1840s and 1850s had a vertical stem with a hand-wheel at the top of each car. A brakeman turning the wheel (as illustrated at left) would wind up a chain that would force the brake shoes against the wheels.

Freight cars were equipped with ladders up their sides and walkways on their tops to permit a brakeman to handle four or five cars at a time by jumping from one car to the next while the train was moving. Yes, it was an extremely hazardous job! When he needed the brakes applied, the engineer would use the whistle to call "down brakes," and the brakemen would begin to scramble to their tasks.

When the brakes were to be released, the engineer would whistle again, and the brakemen would tighten up on the brakewheel enough to kick out the locking ratchet and then let the chain unwind and the brake shoes go slack. With all the momentum and weight, brakes were slow to affect the speed of the train, so the engineer and crew had to anticipate their needs well in advance. It would often take one or two minutes to slow and stop even a modestly moving 15-MPH train.

WESTINGHOUSE AND THE AIR BRAKE

American folklore attributes the idea for air brakes to a train ride between Troy and Schenectady, New York, in 1866 by the 20-year-old George Westinghouse. His journey was delayed by a wreck on the track ahead, when two freight trains had collided head-on in broad daylight because the brakemen could not crank down the handbrakes quickly enough to stop in time. The incident reportedly prompted Westinghouse to begin considering ways to more efficiently apply brakes on moving trains. Within three years he had invented the air brake.

This makes a nice story and has elements of the truth, but in reality Westinghouse was not the first person to experiment with air brakes. He was, however, the one who took some existing elements and ideas and put them together in a truly workable form and wound up creating a manufacturing company that is still one of the corporate giants of the railway supply industry.

While experimenting with both steam and electricity in the mid-1860s for possible breaking systems, Westinghouse read a magazine article describing the construction of the Mont Cenis Tunnel through the Italian Alps, which used a 3,000-foot pipeline to carry compressed air to the rock drills on the working face. This proved that compressed air could be efficiently transmitted in a pipeline that was much longer than a typical freight train.

The air compressor had been developed during the same time period as the steam engine in the 1820s in England, but by the 1860s there had still been no significant industrial use of compressed air in North America. Westinghouse recognized compressed air as a weightless but potentially powerful means to control a train brake, and on April 13, 1869, he was granted U.S. Patent 5504 for his first practical design. He was only 23 years old at the time.

This first "straight air" system had its drawbacks, however, since it used air from the locomotive's reservoir fed into the "trainline" (air-brake line) to directly activate the brakes on the cars. If the trainline should break for any reason, all braking was lost. Something more fail-safe was needed.

By 1873 Westinghouse's engineers had developed the improved system that remains to this day as one of the most significant safety inventions of all time. In the new system, each car carried a reservoir which contained enough air for two or three applications to the brake cylinder. A "triple-valve" under each car on the trainline would charge each reservoir and keep the brakes released as long as pressure was maintained in the line. When the engineer wanted to apply the brakes, he would vent air from the line (rather than pump air into it), and the triple-valves would shift position and discharge the reservoirs into the brake cylinders. This way, if the train should break in two and the trainline rupture, both segments of the broken train would go immediately into a full emergency stop. The brakes could not be released until the pressure was restored to the trainline and the reservoirs were recharged.

Westinghouse's technological break-through was greeted with widespread industry apathy. Air brakes were fine for passenger trains, where the car fleets were small, but for the thousands of everyday freight cars, the hand brakes worked quite well for the money, thank you. The motive-power departments were not interested in hanging expensive and maintenance-prone air pumps on their locomotives—brakes were the responsibility of the car departments.

The industry wallowed in indecision on the matter of brakes until 1888, when Westinghouse introduced the improved "Quick-Acting" brake system that would become the industry standard.

Acceptance and conversion was still slow, however, because of the sheer number of freight cars and expense involved. This transition period was a troublesome time as well, because the conversion to knuckle couplers was also in its full glory, and the nationwide fleet was about as non-standard as it could get.

Trackwork was improving, however, and train speeds were increasing. Better track permitted bigger and heavier freight cars, and bigger cars could handle the same tonnage with fewer actual cars—and fewer sets of expensive air-brake gear. The economies of scale were beginning to work in favor of knuckle couplers and the Westinghouse air brake.

The Railway Safety Appliance Act passed by Congress in 1893 mandated both knuckle couplers and air brakes. The robust nature of these two safety devices, however, permitted North America to develop the finest railroad system the world would ever see.

ROBBER BARONS AND RIVALRIES

The rapid growth of the railroad network following the Civil War, highlighted by the completion of the first transcontinental railroad in May 1869 (a cooperation and competition between the Union Pacific building west from Omaha, Nebraska, and the Central Pacific building east from Sacramento, California), was the largest industrial enterprise in the history of mankind. And it brought out both the best and worst elements of mankind. The government encouraged the railroads

BELOW LEFT: For safety and ease of parts replacement, a modern "26L" airbrake system was applied to Canadian Pacific 4-6-2 No. 2317 at the Steamtown National Historic Site. The engineer's hand is on the "independent" brake valve that controls the brakes only on the locomotive, while the larger handle above it is the automatic "big air" that controls the brakes on the entire train.

BELOW: This diagram, titled "The Westinghouse Plain Automatic Air Brake, 1872," depicts the system that revolutionized the railroad industry and made possible the long and heavy trains that we know today. At the right, a steam-driven reciprocating pump aboard the locomotive compresses the air, which is piped through the train by flexible hoses between the cars. The "triple valve" in each car stores compressed air in the reservoir, which is used to actuate the brake cylinders when the pressure in the trainline is reduced by the engineer actuating the master valve in the cab. The system is "fail safe" in that a break in the trainline will cause all brakes to automatically apply at full strength.
RAILFAN & RAILROAD *COLLECTION*

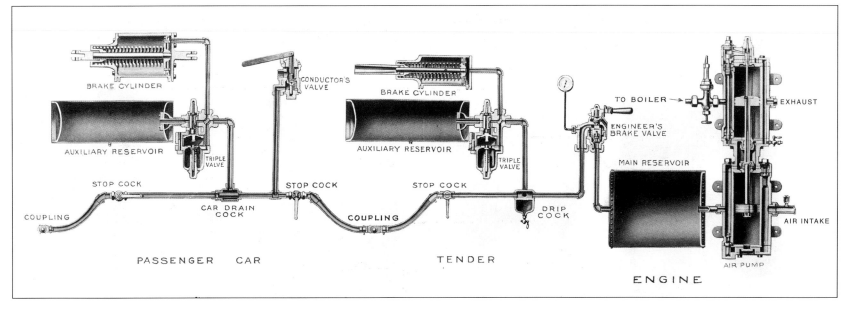

to build into the prairies by offering free land for the right-of-way and substantial paths of land on either side that the railroads could sell.

There was an enormous amount of money to be made, and financiers and industrialists were quick to take advantage of the situation. They sold the rich farmland at bargain prices that were nearly 100 percent profit, created towns along their tracks, and moved immigrants into the countryside by the trainload. Then they supplied the new population with building supplies and other necessities and carried the resulting crops to markets back East.

Railroad companies and bankers raised money for construction by selling stock, and the money-changers elevated stock manipulation to levels of knavery never seen before on such a scale. Ebenezer Scrooge and Jacob Marley would have been proud of them. Railroad financiers like J. P. Morgan, Jim Fisk, Cornelius Vanderbilt, and

Jay Gould often yielded more raw economic power than the federal government, and their intense competition and rivalries resulted in their becoming known as "rail barons." In addition to stock manipulation, the rival companies would try to drive each other out of business with "rate wars" where freight tariffs would be temporarily reduced to hurt the competition or force them to sell out— but once a monopoly was established, the rates could be driven up almost without limit. The railroads' economic power could be used to the advantage of or against other industries, where favored customers would get lower rates for the same services.

Not all railroad magnates were scoundrels, however, for men like E. H. Harriman of the Union Pacific and James J. Hill of the Great Northern created great systems based on sound engineering and honest business practices. All of the corruption and financial rough-housing in the 1870s and

After dropping down the length of the Baltimore & Ohio's famous 17-Mile Grade in 1976, the brake shoes and wheels are hot, and this heavy coal train is surrounded by blue smoke as it crosses the Potomac River at Luke, Maryland.

1880s, however, left in its wake a rapidly expanding network of railroads that was literally creating a new nation out of the landscape.

TIME FOR A CHANGE

By the 1880s, the railroads were affecting daily life all across the country. With the development of the telegraph in the 1860s, the railroads had been among the first to promote instant telecommunication. The same telegraph lines that the railroads used for train dispatching could also keep remote communities in touch with the rest of the country.

On November 18, 1883, the railroads even changed everyone's concept of time. Until then, each community had maintained its own local "sun time" by calculating noon from the sun passage directly overhead at its zenith. In the latitude of Chicago, noon shifted westward by one minute every 13 miles. Philadelphia was five minutes behind New York and five minutes ahead of Baltimore. Since train dispatching required an absolute standard for time, this was not only inconvenient, it was downright dangerous!

In 1872, at age 26, William F. Allen became the editor of the *Official Guide of the Railways*, which was a compendium of timetables of every common-carrier railroad. The problem of the nation's more than 50 time zones made his job complex beyond all reason. In 1881 he began to explore ways of making "railroad time" a national standard. Since the 1700s, sailors had been navigating by the longitudes, and the U.S. covered roughly 60 degrees of longitude, or four hours. While there had been proposals to use the longitudes as standard time borders, they were inconveniently aligned for already established communities and "spheres of influence." The result would have been chaotic.

William F. Allen decided to draw his own border lines, keeping important railroad junctions together and avoiding any densely populated areas. With no governmental authority, the railroad network promoted Allen's idea and set November 18, 1883, for its implementation. His system of four Time Zones (Eastern, Central, Mountain, and Pacific) was so well thought out and resolved so many daily inconveniences that the vast majority of the country went along willingly. Over the next few years the borders were adjusted, but the basic system remained intact. As you look at the digital clock today on your VCR, you are reading the time established by a railroad man in 1883!

The railroads populated the American West by offering low-cost land, bringing in settlers, and then supplying them with the stuff of civilization while transporting their harvest to market. The entire process is summed up in this 1880 photo of the Northern Pacific at Mandan, North Dakota. Homesteaders are loading their wagons with supplies brought by boxcar. In the left distance is a classic roundhouse, and at right is the NP freight depot. RAILFAN & RAILROAD COLLECTION.

In an era of robber barons and ruthless financiers, a few names stand out for their dedication to solid business practices. The Great Northern Railway was pushed across the Pacific Northwest in the 1880s by James J. Hill, who became known as the "Empire Builder," a term of respect and not derision. In 1967 a pair of Great Northern's Electro-Motive GP20s is westbound on the main line out of Minneapolis, passing under the Minneapolis, Northfield & Southern bridge, with a train of empty refrigerator cars, likely bound for the orchards of Washington state.

REGULATION, DEPRESSION, AND WAR

In February 1887 the U.S. Congress passed the Interstate Commerce Act, which created the Interstate Commerce Commission (ICC) to regulate and standardize the rate practices of all common-carriers like the railroads and waterways. This was the federal government's first taste of industrial blood through a regulatory agency, and the politicians found it a heady experience to which they would soon become addicted.

By the turn of the century, the railroads were becoming well organized, standardized, and regulated. Trackwork and signaling standards were improving rapidly, and locomotive and rolling-stock technology were making great strides in capacity and reliability. Freight cars were shifting from wood construction to steel, and trains were getting larger, heavier, faster, and yet safer.

The local station agent became the focus of commerce of nearly every community, and armies of clerks and accountants with ink pens, ledger books, and telegraph communications were keeping track of the hundreds of thousands of freight-car movements and business transactions.

World War I presented the railroad industry with a real emergency situation, as standardization had created one nationwide network, but corporate squabbling was severely impacting its efficiency. Emptied freight cars were slow to return to their home roads, and the variations in car construction and repair parts made maintenance an expensive and time-consuming process.

The U.S. entered the conflict on April 6, 1917, and before the end of the year, the railroads were becoming paralyzed by the strain. On December 26, 1917, President Woodrow Wilson placed the railroads under the control of the federal government through a newly created agency, the United States Railroad Administration. The agency was headed by William G. McAdoo, a former railroader and now Secretary of the Treasury. The USRA did not confiscate or nationalize the privately owned systems but essentially "rented" them by guaranteeing each

The period between the first and second world wars was, in railroading, known as the "Standard Era," when the railroad industry achieved its modern size and capacity and became the true industrial backbone of the nation while the automobile, highway truck, and airplane were in their infancies. Nearly everything and everyone moved by rail, as typified by this scene on the New York, New Haven & Hartford Railroad at East Braintree, Massachusetts, on October 6, 1928, with a road-worthy heavy 2-6-0 on a typical local freight train of the era. BOB'S PHOTOS, BRIAN SOLOMON COLLECTION

company fair earnings. Competition was eliminated, and wages were raised.

McAdoo assembled blue-ribbon mechanical committees to develop standard designs for locomotives and rolling stock that could be used anywhere in the country. More than 2,000 locomotives and 50,000 freight cars were built to USRA standards under government order. The task was done so well, that the "USRA Standard" locomotives and cars continued to be manufactured for decades to follow.

The war ended on November 11, 1918, and the railroads were returned to private management on March 1, 1920. The now-prosperous railways were still the steel backbone of America, and competition from the highway, automobile, and airplane was not considered a serious threat.

Then the bottom fell out. The stock market crashed in 1929, and the nation fell into the Great Depression. Industry collapsed, traffic plummeted, and unemployment was rampant. The strongest railroads just tightened their belts and survived on their recently strengthened infrastructure. The less fortunate railroads simply collapsed into bankruptcy.

In the mid-1930s, a bright spot appeared in the form of the diesel-electric passenger "streamliner." Lightweight and economical, they caught the attention of the general pubic. Almost invisible to the public, however, in the freight yards, switching locomotives born of the same diesel technology were forecasting a drastic change in the character of the freight train.

By the time the U.S. entered World War II in December 1941, the America's railway system had "come of age." The technology was reliable and rugged. The Great Depression had thinned the ranks of some of the weaker systems, so the vast remaining network was strong. Steam was still the king, although electric motive power was established in areas where it was economically viable, and the new diesel-electric locomotive was already showing the way to the future.

The lessons of World War I had been learned and applied, and no government interference was needed this time around. The privately owned and home-managed railroads handled the staggering wartime traffic with a robust energy that is difficult to imagine. For America's railroads, this was their finest hour.

The railroad industry was ready for World War II and survived the conflict without government takeover. The diesel-electric had been introduced in the late 1930s and proved its efficiency during the war. As soon as peace returned, the railroads were eager to dieselize. From 1945 to 1960 steam and diesel power worked side-by-side as the new technology began to push aside the old. On December 31, 1956, a Pennsylvania Railroad M1-b 4-8-2 eases up the approach to Bank Tower just west of Enola Yard in Harrisburg while a fast-moving manifest with new GP9 diesels sweeps past on the outer main track. The "handrails" atop the diesels are actually induction telephone antennas, which were the precursors of the portable radios that would revolutionize railroading even more than the locomotives themselves. JOHN DZIOBKO

The classic American freight steam locomotive was the 2-8-2, a wheel arrangement created in 1897 as an export for Japan, thereby getting the name "Mikado." These powerful and versatile machines were ideal for 40–50-MPH operation and could handle an 80-car train on level track. They were used on almost every railroad in the country, and here in 1957, in the last days of the steam era, a veteran Illinois Central "Mike" was working the cement plant at Lehigh, Illinois. —JOHN SZWAJKART

3

What Makes a *Freight* *Locomotive?*

he earliest locomotives were simple machines designed to replace a horse or mule in moving wagons or carriages over the rails. As early as the 1840s, however, steam locomotives were beginning to be designed for specific duties. The size of the boiler would determine the overall "power" of the locomotive, but it could be applied for either speed or pulling power, depending on the size of the cylinders and driving wheels.

In 1939, the Electro-Motive Corporation introduced the first true road freight diesel-electric locomotive in a four-unit demonstrator set numbered 103. In 1989, half of that original "FT" set was restored by the Electro-Motive Division of General Motors to celebrate the FT's 50th anniversary with a gala open house at the locomotive factory in LaGrange, Illinois. Fifty years of "F-units" are represented by the lineup (left to right) of the 1350-hp FT 103 of 1939, the 6600-hp Union Pacific DDA40X 6936 of 1969, the 3800-hp UP SD60M 6200 of 1989, and the 3600-hp Santa Fe FP45 101 of 1967. Unlike a steam locomotive, which has to be designed from the ground up for freight or passenger service, diesels can be tailored to either simply by changing gear ratios and adding "head end power" for the passenger cars. Of these, the FP45 is actually a passenger unit, and there were FTs equipped for passenger duty, as well.

From the 1850s through the 1880s, the 4-4-0 "American Standard" lived up to its name as the universal locomotive for both freight and passenger service. Milwaukee Road 705 was a typical coal-burning 4-4-0 of that era. MILWAUKEE ROAD HISTORICAL ASSOCIATION ARCHIVES

Large-diameter driving wheels ("tall" drivers) were ideal for speed, while smaller driving wheels were slower but more sure-footed and could apply much more pulling power to the rails.

In the years up through the Civil War, the most popular type of locomotive in North America was the "American Standard" 4-4-0. This simple but rugged design could be built with drivers and cylinders of differing sizes, but most were an optimum balance between speed and power that made them ideal "dual service" locomotives that were fast enough for passenger service on the poor track of that era and still powerful enough to be effective freight engines.

WHEEL ARRANGEMENTS

As locomotive designs became more numerous following the Civil War, the industry needed a convenient way to identify the different general types. The configuration of the wheels was an obvious answer. Locomotives usually had three groups of wheels beneath the boiler: a pilot truck comprised of small non-powered wheels, then a

ABOVE: This Milwaukee Road 2-8-0 (two-wheel lead truck, eight drivers, and no trailing truck), built in 1904, shows the "low" drivers that were typical of a slow freight locomotive. MILWAUKEE ROAD HISTORICAL ASSOCIATION ARCHIVES

RIGHT: Former Canadian Pacific 4-6-2 1293, in excursion service on the Ohio Central in 1997, is a typical passenger locomotive with moderately "high" drivers. The four-wheel pilot truck is characteristic of a high-speed engine for freight or passenger service.

introduced in 1893 when Baldwin moved the firebox completely behind the driving wheels on a large 2-4-2 to make it wider and deeper for more efficient fuel combustion.

The same boiler could be used on either a freight or passenger locomotive, depending on the size and number of drivers that were placed beneath it. A classic example of this is the Pennsylvania Railroad Class K4s 4-6-2 Pacific type and L1s 2-8-2 Mikado of 1914–1928. Both had the same trailing truck, but the 4-6-2 had three sets of 80-inch drivers and a four-wheel pilot truck, while the 2-8-2 had four sets of 62-inch drivers and a single-axle pilot truck in the same overall space. These were very successful locomotives, and the Pennsy had 425 identical K4s passenger 4-6-2s and 574 L1s freight 2-8-2s!

The four-wheel trailing truck was introduced by the Lima Locomotive Works in 1925 when it greatly enlarged the firebox on a large 2-8-2 freight engine to create the first 2-8-4. The huge fireboxes and four-wheel trailing trucks were soon applied to

Between 1914 and 1928 the Pennsylvania Railroad bought or built themselves 574 of these L1s 2-8-2s, and the only survivor is the 520 at the Pennsylvania State Railroad Museum in Strasburg. In an example of standardization, the PRR used the same boiler over tall drivers for 425 of its K4s passenger 4-6-2s.

An Erie Railroad 2-10-2 is deep in the Poncono Mountains of Pennsylvania near Forest City circa 1940. This wheel arrangement was known as the "Santa Fe" type, account of it being developed for that famous company, which owned most of the 2-10-2s built. Locomotives of this type were used in service where 2-8-2s (Mikados) would have been used, but where a bit more tractive effort—albeit at the expense of speed—was necessary. BERT PENNYPACKER, ANDOVER JUNCTION PUBLICATIONS COLLECTION

series of rod-connected driving wheels followed by a trailing truck made up of more small non-powered wheels. These "wheel arrangements" were identified with a number for each wheel group, using only even digits, as a single axle with two wheels was identified with the number "2," and so forth. Thus a freight engine with a single-axle two-wheeled pilot truck, six drivers (three on each side), and a two-wheeled trailing truck would be a 2-6-2. The American Standard, with its two-axle, four-wheel pilot truck, four driving wheels and no trailing truck was a 4-4-0—and the zero was verbalized as "oh," making the American a "four-four-oh." As each new wheel arrangement was created, it was also given a name—the 4-6-0 was simply a "Ten-Wheeler," while the first 2-8-2 "Mikado" was built for export to Japan, whose Emperor was known as "The Mikado."

This system was standardized by Frederick M. Whyte, a mechanical engineer for the New York Central & Hudson River, and adopted in 1901 by the Railway Master Mechanics Association. The Whyte System identified only the wheel arrangement and made no reference to the size, speed, or service characteristics of a locomotive. One could, however, draw some general conclusions from wheel arrangements. Locomotives with a two-wheel pilot truck tended to be low-drivered freight engines, while those with a four-wheel pilot truck tended to be passenger or dual-service engines.

The trailing truck would not reflect the type of service for a locomotive, but it would be a good indicator of the overall size of the machine. Locomotives with no trailing trucks generally had small fireboxes either between or above the driving wheels. The two-wheel trailing truck was

One of the most perfectly designed freight locomotives of all time was the Nickel Plate's famous 2-8-4 Berkshires. Here in 1956, the 764 was westbound near Hammond, Indiana, with a typical Nickel Plate fast freight. The railroad had 80 of these machines that could cruise comfortably at 70 MPH with a mile of freight behind them. RUSS PORTER

both freight and passenger engines in the next few years as the concept of high-horsepower "Super Power" swept the industry and led to the creation of the most powerful steam locomotives ever built.

The classic freight locomotives from the Civil War onward were the 2-6-0 Mogul, 2-8-0 Consolidation, 2-10-0 Decapod, 2-6-2 Prairie, 2-8-2 Mikado, 2-10-2 Santa Fe, 2-8-4 Berkshire, and 2-10-4 Texas types. Modern dual-service locomotives that saw extensive freight duty include the 4-8-2 Mountain type and 4-8-4 Northern. Even the 4-6-2 Pacific, typically a passenger engine, was used by many railroads in freight service.

ARTICULATEDS AND MALLETS

Shortly after 1900, locomotives were reaching the limit in the number of driving wheels that could be placed under a boiler and still be able to negotiate curves. Five sets of low drivers was about as long a "rigid wheelbase" as the railroad

system could accommodate. In 1888, however, a Swiss designer named Anatole Mallet had created a locomotive with a hinge on its underframe and two sets of cylinders and driving wheels. The "rear engine" was rigidly attached to the boiler and firebox, while the "front engine" could swing from side to side from its rear pivot.

This "articulated" concept was brought to the U.S. in 1903 in the form of a powerful but slow 0-6-6-0 for the Baltimore & Ohio, which was used as a pusher locomotive on heavy coal trains on mountain grades. The B&O 2400, "Old Maud," was a "compound articulated" in that the rear engine used hot steam directly from the boiler and used its exhaust steam to drive the front engine—much larger cylinders on the front engine gave both sets the same pulling power in spite of the difference in steam heat and pressure.

By 1914 the compound articulated was developing into huge and powerful, if somewhat slow and ponderous, freight locomotives. These "compound" Mallets (pronounced MAL-leys) were very popular on mountainous railroads and for heavy coal trains, where their top working speed was about 35 MPH.

In 1924, Alco built a group of huge 2-8-8-2 "simple" articulateds for the Chesapeake & Ohio which had boilers big enough to supply all four cylinders directly with high-pressure hot steam. Over the next decade, the simple articulated grew into the 2-8-8-4 and 2-6-6-4 for freight service and 4-6-6-4 for dual service (with 70-inch drivers, the 2-6-6-4s and 4-6-6-4s were capable of sustained speeds over 70 MPH).

By the 1940s, the articulateds had grown to the awesome 2-6-6-6 Alleghenies for freight service on the C&O and Virginian, and the Union Pacific's "Big Boy" 4-8-8-4s. The Big Boys would go down in history as the largest steam locomotives ever built, although the honor for "most powerful" was subject to interpretation as to just how that "power" was measured. No one could argue, however, that the Big Boy was the biggest.

FREIGHT DIESELS

Electricity had been used to power locomotives since the 1890s, but the cost of installing overhead wire or a trackside third rail made it economically viable only in areas of great traffic density, where smoke was a hazard (such as in a long tunnel), and occasionally in mountain-railroad application. In 1885, Frank Sprague had developed the "nose hung" electric traction motor that rode directly on the driving axle to which it was

One of the most powerful boilers ever applied to a steam locomotive was carried by the Chesapeake & Ohio's 2-6-6-6 "Alleghenies," built by the Lima Locomotive Works in the 1940s. The 1647 is shown at Fostoria, Ohio, en route from Columbus to Toledo in June 1950.
J. J. YOUNG JR.

Electric Freight Motors

The Milwaukee Road had 655 miles of 3,000-volt DC electrification on its Pacific Extension. In October 1971, the Milwaukee's first 1915 GE freight motor, E50A, is working as a mid-train helper on eastbound freight 264 as it drops downgrade through Saltese, Montana, after climbing over St. Paul Pass.

The electric motor was invented in 1830 in Albany, New York, about the same time that George Stephenson in England was building the *John Bull* for the Camden & Amboy. A hundred years later these two events combined to produce the greatest mainline electrification in America, the Pennsylvania Railroad's "Northeast Corridor." Heavy-duty generators and traction motors became available around the turn of the century, and electric locomotives quickly proved themselves rugged, reliable, and incredibly powerful. But they were also very expensive. The cost of stringing overhead wires or laying third rails to transmit the power was a severely limiting expense, and electrification was restricted to specific areas where it could be put to most economical use. These were generally where passenger service was heavy or where tunnels made smoke a problem. In the first half of the twentieth century, there was little standardization, and the advantages and limitations of alternating current (AC) and direct current (DC) were being resolved through trial-and-error. Today's efficient AC systems were made possible only through the development of solid-state components and computer technology. The Norfolk & Western, Virginian, Great Northern, and Milwaukee Road had main lines that were electrified primarily for freight, but today the only freight handled under wires is on captive industrial operations (page 82).

geared. This simple but rugged system made possible the building of the first electric streetcars.

In 1910, General Electric began building self-propelled railcars using a gasoline engine to power a generator that created electricity for a pair of traction motors. These passenger "doodlebugs" were fairly successful, but GE lost interest and ceased production in 1917. In 1924, however, a little outfit called the Electro-Motive Company opened a workshop in Cleveland, Ohio, to produce gas-electric motorcars. Under EMC, the gas-electric became more powerful and reliable.

Meanwhile, in 1918, GE had applied gas-electric technology to a locomotive using an Ingersoll-Rand diesel instead of a gasoline engine. In 1924 GE put its electrical system with a 300-hp I-R diesel engine into a 60-ton boxcab carbody built by Alco to produce the world's first commercially successful diesel-electric locomotive. Jersey Central 1000 went into freight switching service in New York City, where steam locomotives had been banned because of their smoke nuisance.

The diesel engine, invented by Dr. Rudolf Diesel in Germany in 1892, is simpler and more rugged than a gasoline engine and can burn a wide range of lower-grade and less-expensive fuel. Diesels tend to be much larger, heavier, and slower-running than gasoline engines, which makes them ideal for locomotive work.

The diesel engines found in early locomotives built by Ingersoll-Rand were ponderous six-cylinder inline machines using the four-stroke cycle like a gasoline engine. However, in 1934 Electro-Motive—which in 1930 had become a subsidiary of General Motors and teamed up with the Winton Engine Company—introduced a revolutionary lightweight two-stroke-cycle diesel. The Winton "201A" was designed for use on both submarines and locomotives and was available in a 600-hp 8-cylinder inline and 900-hp 12-cylinder and 1,200-hp 16-cylinder "V" configurations.

But First, the Streamliners

With a typical freight steam locomotive already in the 3000-hp range, even a 1,200-hp diesel-electric wasn't exactly ready to take over the nation's railroads. But it could grab the headlines. Electro-Motive put a new Winton 201A engine in a shiny stainless-steel streamliner and immediately caught the nation's attention. *Zephyr* 9900 was built by the Edward G. Budd Manufacturing Company for the Chicago, Burlington & Quincy. This little three-car speedster raced nonstop from Denver to Chicago on May 26, 1934, covering 1,015 miles in just over 13 hours, averaging over 77 MPH. EMC definitely knew how to make headlines!

The lightweight streamliners, however, were severely limited in weight and passenger capacity, which seriously limited their potential. Electro-Motive's design engineer Dick Dilworth knew that it would take at least 3,600-hp to replace a modern steam locomotive on a full-sized passenger train. He envisioned placing two 900-hp 201A engines in one boxcab carbody to produce an 1,800-hp unit—and two of those, linked electrically to operate together, would create a 3,600-hp locomotive.

Each of Dilworth's box-cabs rode two four-wheel trucks, each of which carried two traction motors. (In the established terminology of electric locomotives, this four-wheel configuration with two adjacent traction motors was known as a "B"

The first commercially successful diesel-electric locomotives were a group of 60-ton, 300-hp box-cabs produced by the American Locomotive Company (Alco), General Electric, and Ingersoll-Rand in the mid-1920s. Ingersoll-Rand kept the 90, built in December 1926, as its Phillipsburg, New Jersey, plant switcher and in 1970 donated it to the Ford Museum in Dearborn, Michigan, where it is shown on display in January 1999.

INSET: *Nearly a decade after the ugly little box-cab switchers had proved the reliability of the diesel engine, it was the futuristic "streamliner" that put the diesel locomotive into the public's eye. Less than a year after the CB&Q Zephyr 9900 made headlines on May 26, 1934, with a nonstop sprint from Denver to Chicago, the Boston & Maine and Maine Central introduced the nearly identical* Flying Yankee *for service between Boston and Bangor, Maine. The little shovel-nose train was displayed at the Edaville Railroad in South Carver, Massachusetts, in the 1970s and as of 2001 was undergoing restoration at Crawford Notch, New Hampshire, for possible excursion service.*

The diesel locomotive that killed the steam engine was the Electro-Motive model FT, introduced in 1939. Powered by EMC's new 16-cylinder, 1,350-hp "567" diesel engine, the FT was initially offered only as a two-unit cab-and-booster set like the first two units on this Santa Fe train on the "Joint Line" at Larkspur, Colorado, on January 16, 1961. Once the matter was resolved of not having to assign a fireman to each "locomotive" as per the steam-era labor contracts, the diesels could be assembled of individual units in any combination, such as the single FT cab unit trailing this set. The FT proved itself during the World War II, and immediately after hostilities ceased, the builders could not manufacture diesels fast enough to meet the railroads' demands. MAINLINE PHOTOS

truck, and the locomotive wheel arrangement was "B-B.") The two-unit prototype, numbered 511 and 512, was built in 1935. And it worked.

The Santa Fe selected selected Dilworth's box-cabs to power its new *Super Chief* streamliner between Chicago and Los Angeles. The 1935 *Super Chief* was the first full-sized luxury passenger train to be designed from the onset to use diesel-electric power.

Although they had tolerated the streetcar-like control cabs on the little *Zephyr*s, the locomotive crews of heavyweight passenger trains, accustomed to riding behind the "protection" of a 200-ton, 70-foot boiler, were wary of their vulnerable position at the front of the box-cabs, where they would be the first to arrive on the scene of any mishap. So Electro-Motive went to work to move the engineer away from the front window. This resulted in an overall larger locomotive in what

became known as the "covered wagon" carbody with an engineer's control cab at one end.

Realizing the market potential for this new locomotive, General Motors put its automotive design talents to work on styling this new stream-liner. The result was an absolute classic of Art Deco design, with an elegantly slanted nose and smoothly contoured front cab windows. This was not only a fast and powerful locomotive, it looked like a fast and powerful locomotive!

Knowing that it would take two or three of its new diesel-electrics to equal or surpass the performance of a steam locomotive, EMD adopted the concept of optional cab and booster units. The cab units, known as "A-units," had the engineer's control cab at one end, while the booster "B-units" had no cab whatsoever and would simply be inexpensive "building blocks" to increase the horsepower behind the cab unit.

The True Freight Diesel

The Winton 201A was a good diesel engine, but it had been designed as a compromise between submarine and locomotive needs and had some inherent weight-versus-strength problems that made it difficult to manufacture and required careful maintenance in regular service. Electro-Motive had the backing of GM to build a new diesel prime mover from scratch.

The new EMC diesel engine was designed from the ground up as a simpler and more rugged version of the 201A with a high degree of standardization and parts interchangeability. The new "Model 567" was named for its cubic inch displacement per cylinder. With the V-12 rated at 1000 hp, the new 567 immediately replaced the similar-sized 201A's in the passenger units, which boosted a two-unit set from 3,600 to 4,000 hp. And a three-unit A-B-A set of the new E3s at 6,000 hp could outperform any steam locomotive ever built.

While passenger trains got the glamour and glory, EMC knew that the really big market was the 50,000 steam freight locomotives that were in service at that time. The V-16 version of the new 567 could deliver 1,350 hp, and a four-unit set would yield 5,400 hp, which was a match for almost any steam locomotive.

The new "FT" freight diesel would be made up of a cab and booster permanently linked by a solid drawbar instead of a coupler. These would be shorter versions of the carbodies used by the passenger E-units. On the new freight units, however, there was no room available for the long, slanted nose, so EMC shortened it to a pleasingly rounded "bulldog" contour that also turned out to be a classic of engineering styling.

The first FT, the four-unit A-B-B-A demonstrator set numbered 103, was completed in November 1939 and, wearing a handsome olive green and Dulux gold paint job, it set off on a nearly year-long tour of 83,764 miles over 20 railroads in 38 states. The 103 proved to be rugged and reliable and capable of handling any assignment. When the trip was completed in October 1940, although the industry didn't know it, the steam locomotive was dead. All that remained was a 20-year task of burying the corpse.

Electro-Motive was formally absorbed into General Motors on January 1, 1940, as the Electro-Motive Division, better known simply as "EMD." The 103 was just wrapping up its tour when the Santa Fe placed the first order for production FT's,

and by the end of World War II, the Santa Fe had acquired the nation's largest fleet of FTs, 155 cabs and 165 boosters. With a total production of 1,190 units by the end of 1945, the FT was credited with contributing heavily to handling the wartime traffic emergency. In 1946 the FT was upgraded to 1,500 horsepower per unit as the new "F3," and the assault on the steam monopoly was in full stride.

The two biggest steam locomotive builders, Baldwin and Alco, had seen the writing on the wall and had begun to develop their own diesel programs in the late 1930s when the threat from Electro-Motive had become apparent. Alco had teamed up with GE for electrical support and responded with a twin-engine passenger unit at 2,000 hp and was engineering a freight unit like the FT when the war interrupted its plans. After the war, both Alco-GE and Baldwin-Westinghouse responded with 1,500-hp models to match the F3, while another firm, Fairbanks, Morse & Company (later, Fairbanks-Morse), entered the fray with a 2,000-hp dual-service unit using a unique opposed piston, two-stroke engine that had proven itself in wartime submarines. But EMD was still leading the pack by a country mile.

By the late 1940s a standard electrical system had been adopted that permitted units of any manufacturer to be incorporated into a locomotive consist. This multiple-unit system, generally referred to simply as "m.u.," was the key to the success of the diesel locomotive, as any number of units could be combined together under the control of one engineer to match the power requirements of virtually any job. Two diesels could replace a 2-8-2 on a local freight, while six could be "m.u.'ed" together to outperform the mightiest 4-8-8-4. And the six-unit diesel set could operate on many lines that could not begin to handle the sheer weight of such a large steam locomotive.

Although in the 1940s all steam locomotives were still being designed to meet the specific operating needs of each customer, the diesel builders were offering standard "off the shelf" models that could do the same jobs better and cheaper. It was the EMD philosophy of offering a few standard but versatile models and backing them up with factory technical support, parts warehouses, and worker training that sold the railroads on diesel power over the proven but labor-intensive steam locomotive.

The diesel-electric had another advantage in that it was an "automatic" machine that did not require constant human attention like a steam

ABOVE: *The success of EMC's FT prompted Alco to respond in 1945 its own 1,500-hp "covered wagon" freight unit, the FA1, powered by its own new diesel engine, the Model 244. In 1965 Alco FA2 588 leads the Lehigh Valley's connection from Binghamton, New York, into Sayre, Pennsylvania.* JIM SHAUGHNESSY

ABOVE RIGHT: *As EMC was hawking its FT diesel in the early 1940s, both Alco and Baldwin were still designing and selling new steam locomotives. Immediately after the war, Baldwin got into the road freight diesel market, and in 1949 it introduced its distinctive "Sharknose" carbody. On September 20, 1952, a set of Pennsylvania Railroad DR4-4-1500 "Sharks" rolls freight through Bradford, Ohio.* R. D. ACTON SR.

locomotive, which would run itself out of fuel and water if not properly manned. And the diesel could run all day on a tank of fuel and not need to visit the roundhouse or ashpit every few hours to have its fire cleaned or machinery lubricated. Whereas even a modern steam locomotive generally could not run more than about 250 miles before being pulled off the train and serviced, a diesel set could run a thousand miles or more and then continue on with nothing more than a quick refueling.

A yard that once required five steam switchers could be worked effectively with two diesels. By 1960, for instance, the Illinois Central had replaced 1,166 steam locomotives with just over 600 diesels handling the same traffic.

The Road-Switcher

The earliest diesels had been relatively small switching locomotives in boxcar-like carbodies. By the mid-1930s the box-cab carbody had been abandoned in favor of a simple girder frame with a cab at one end and the engine compartment covered by a narrow hood that left walkways on either side. Since all the strength was in the frame, the hood was just a flimsy shell to keep out the weather, and doors on the sides could be opened up for

easy access to the engine and electrical equipment for maintenance.

In 1940, Alco-GE extended the frame of its 1,000-hp switch engine and added a short hood behind the cab. The unit rode on a pair of four-wheel, two-motor road trucks and had the necessary electrical capacity for high-speed road service. This "RS1" was described as a "road-switcher," and the idea was a good one. Although it was a bit shy on sheer horsepower, the RS1 would be very handy for branchline and local freight service, as well as yard work and even secondary passenger runs .

After World War II, Alco-GE introduced the 1,500-hp RS2 with its new lightweight "Model 244" engine. Born in 1946, the RS2 was the first true road-switcher with the horsepower that could match a mainline road unit like the EMD F3.

The "Geep"

In 1949 EMD still had no offering in the road-switcher market. Although the official GM corporate history describes Dick Dilworth coming up with the idea for his new road-switcher as a pristine vision, he was undoubtedly aware of the Alco RS1 and RS2 and previous EMD road-worthy switchers and transfer units. He simply took the machinery of a 1,500-hp road unit and placed it on a girder underframe like a switcher in the same general arrangement as the Alco RS1 and RS2. He made no effort, however, to provide visibility over the hood, which was for all practical purposes useless, anyhow. This permitted him to use a stronger and thicker underframe and gave plenty of room overhead for the exhaust manifolds and cooling radiators and fans. The GP was born.

The "GP" designation meant "General Purpose," and the phonetics naturally led to the same adaptation of the popular Army "Jeep" pronunciation, although the industry press picked up the spelling as "Geep." (Army Jeeps had likewise been designated as "General Purpose" or "GP" vehicles and the GP pronunciation altered to "Jeep.") Since the new GP was the road-switcher version of the F7 freight unit, Dilworth's new locomotive was designated a GP7. The first unit rolled out in October 1949 as EMD demonstrator 922, and in August 1950 it was sold to the Chicago & North Western as the 1518 (this unit is now preserved at the Illinois Railway Museum at Union, Illinois).

Between October 1949 and December 1953, EMD cranked out 1,299 of Dilworth's GP7s and then upgraded it up to 1,750 hp with the nearly identical GP9, which sold 3,969 more! The utilitarian Geep had redefined the diesel freight locomotive. The road-switcher offered the same power as the covered-wagon road units and added the visibility and flexibility of a switcher. By adding steam generators for train heating, a number of railroads used Geeps to haul passenger trains as well, underscoring the "general purpose" designation.

In the Geep, railroading had found its "universal" locomotive, and by 1960 steam was dead with the corpse successfully buried. It was the road-switcher that threw the last shovelful of dirt on the grave.

"Six Motors"

Most freight units in the early 1950s were in the 1,500-hp range, riding on four-wheel trucks. Alco and Baldwin had built some road-switchers on six-wheel A1A trucks with center idler axles to spread the weight on light-rail branch lines, but they still carried only four traction motors.

In the late 1940s, Dilworth investigated the effectiveness of six-motor units. Dilworth and Blomberg developed a superb six-wheel, three-motor "C" truck in 1948 that yielded a 40 percent increase in tractive effort over a comparable B truck. Between 1948 and 1951, Baldwin, Alco-GE, and Fairbanks-Morse began offering six-motor versions of their road-switchers. EMD responded in 1952 with its "Special Duty" six-motor SD7 road-switcher, which at 1,500 hp was essentially a larger version of the GP7. The six-motor units immediately gained a reputation as heavy pullers.

Alco pioneered the concept of adding road trucks and a short hood behind the cab of a 1,000-HP switch engine to create the first true "road-switcher," the RS1 of 1940. The road-switcher became the universal freight locomotive following World War II, and the RS1 stayed in production until 1957, with a total run of 607 units. On March 31, 1957, a pair of Jersey Central RS1s was heading a freight train through Red Bank, New Jersey, on the New York & Long Branch, heading for the CNJ's line into southern New Jersey. JOHN DZIOBKO

In a bizarre example of corporate misdirection, Electro-Motive ignored the Alco concept of the RS1 (and its own earlier experiments in the same format) and attempted in 1948 to create its own version of the road-switcher by starting with the truss frame of the F-unit and trying to carve visibility out of the carbody hood. The peculiar result was the "Branch Line" BL2, shown here as Monon 32, which was "an F-unit with all the working space taken out of it." After building only 59 units, in 1949 EMD's Dick Dilworth went back to the switcher frame format and created the most successful road-switcher of all time, the GP7. Here at the EMD plant at LaGrange, Illinois, on September 15, 1989, FT 103 was posed with Monon BL2 32 from the Kentucky Railway Museum and Chicago & North Western 1518, the first GP7, preserved in operating condition at the Illinois Railway Museum.

The Second Generation

The economic life of a diesel locomotive following World War II was between 12 and 15 years, and by the mid-1950s many of the earlier units were reaching that threshold. Fifteen years of engineering and manufacturing experience had made the diesels of the mid-1950s much more reliable and robust than their predecessors, as well. In 1955 Alco upped the power threshold to 2,400 hp with its big six-motor DL600A, while EMD was marketing its 1,750-hp SD9 of similar size. A horsepower race was about to begin.

In 1959 EMD added a turbocharger to its 16-cylinder 567 engine and introduced the 2,400-hp six-motor SD24 and the 2,000-hp four-motor GP20. These were the first diesels that were designed and marketed to replace diesels, not steam locomotives. The GP20, in particular, was pitched for its ability to do the same work with fewer units. A four-unit set of 1,500-hp F3s could be replaced with three 2,000-hp GP20s. This was the beginning of dieseldom's "second generation."

In 1959 the Santa Fe took delivery of the first production "low nose" hood units in the form of Alco DL600Bs and EMD SD24s. The low-nose units kept the same basic shape and size to the nose and cab except that the hood was "chopped down" to roughly the level of the cab side windows, greatly improving forward visibility. Heavy collision posts inside the nose gave impact protection to the cab, and the set-back position kept the enginemen comfortably away from the point of any collision.

GE and the U25B

The low nose and turbocharger became synonymous with "second generation" for EMD units. In reality, however, the first true second-generation freight locomotive was the U25B, introduced by General Electric in 1959 (with a high short hood, incidentally). GE, a supplier of electrical gear since the early 1900s, had left the road locomotive business when it broke off its marketing agreement with Alco in 1953, but it was preparing to make its own move into the field in a big way.

Beginning with the lusty four-cycle Cooper-Bessemer FDL-16 diesel engine, GE designed a brand new road-switcher from the ground up. This 2,500-hp four-motor unit, called the U25B, made some basic changes in the layout of the equipment on the frame and introduced some innovative new concepts to diesel locomotive design in the area of component arrangement, air filtration, and manufacturing efficiency.

The U25B hit the road in 1959, and soon both EMD and Alco were obliged to similarly redesign the systems of their locomotives. For EMD it began in 1961 with the distinctive 2,250-hp GP30, while Alco made the move with its "Century Series" C424 in 1963.

The Horsepower Race

A diesel-electric locomotive exerts its most effective pulling power at low speed. This is a function of the basic physics of the traction motor, which can apply tremendous torque with

The first high-horsepower six-motor unit was the impressive Fairbanks-Morse Train Master of 1953. At 2,400 hp, this unit was ahead of its time and was short-lived only because it was powered by FM's unique opposed-piston diesel engine that was an "orphan" on most railroads. On June 11, 1962, Wabash Train Master 554 and EMD GP7 460 were on the East Local at Jacksonville, Illinois. DAVE INGLES

Dick Dilworth intentionally designed the GP7 with the high short hood so that a fireman would be required for safe visibility and to avoid becoming a factor in labor disputes. When that matter was resolved, Geeps began to emerge with "chopped noses" like the GP20 leading the Chicago, Burlington & Quincy's symbol freight CGI (Chicago–Grand Island, Nebraska) across the Illinois Central and Milwaukee Road crossing at Mendota, Illinois, in 1965.

Although General Electric had been involved in building electric locomotives and early diesel-electrics since the turn of the century, it had teamed up with Alco to market road units between 1940 and 1953 before striking out on its own. In 1960 it introduced the 2,500-hp four-motor U25B, powered by a turbocharged Cooper-Bessemer four-cycle diesel engine. The U25B was revolutionary in that it was designed new from the ground up and included innovations like inertial air filters and a pressurized carbody to keep the engine room clean. In 1966 a classic U25B was teamed up with an EMD GP35 (which had been designed specifically to match the performance of the U25B) on a westbound Rock Island freight at Wyanet, Illinois. Also note the handful of piggyback trailers on flatcars that were beginning to take over the traditional "boxcar business."

relatively little horsepower. Since total "horsepower" is a combination of power and speed, as the speed increases, the additional available pulling power decreases. To gain more pulling power at greater speed, you need to up the total horsepower. In diesel-electric terms, that means going to a more powerful diesel engine or simply adding more units.

Because of its electric motors, a relatively small switch engine can slowly lug a 100-car freight train in a flat yard, while it takes four 1,500-hp road units to get it up to a 50-MPH track speed. By the mid-1960s, all three manufacturers (EMD, Alco, GE) had their 16-cylinder engines working in the 3,000-hp range, and the six-motor road-switcher proved to be the most efficient combination of total weight, proper number of motors, and optimum horsepower for a modern road locomotive "package."

The 1960s saw EMD and GE begin an all-out battle for market domination. The four-motor units jumped from 2,500 to 3,000 hp, and the six-motors reached 3,600 hp with the EMD SD45 of 1965, which was powered by an awesome 20-cylinder version of the new EMD 645 engine. The high-horsepower units were intended for fast freight service, while a new level of 3,000-hp six-motors, characterized by the EMD SD40, became the universal heavy duty workhorse of the main line.

And while the 3,000-hp four-axle GP40s were the unchallenged speed merchants of most main lines, the 2,000-hp non-turbocharged GP38 began to spread everywhere in the yards, branch lines, and secondary jobs. Covered wagons were disappearing by the late 1960s as the unit replacement programs began to exert their economic benefits.

Shifting the Balance

With the loss of GE as a partner and now facing it as a direct competitor, Alco dropped out of the locomotive business in 1969. Although GE had gotten off to a struggling start, its design innovations and aggressive marketing was beginning to invade EMD's historic territory of market dominance. GE modernized its locomotive factory in Erie, Pennsylvania, and with a good product, vigorous marketing, and creative customer financing, it began to eat away at EMD's historic lead in diesel production, which at one time was over 75 percent of the market.

In the early 1970s, the railroads wanted simple and reliable locomotives, 3,000-hp over six motors, preferably, that would run forever with little or no maintenance. Gas 'em and go! The builders gave them just that, typified by the SD40 and U30C.

Then came the "energy crisis" of 1973 and skyrocketing fuel costs. Now the reliable old gas-guzzlers weren't good enough, and the railroads began screaming for more fuel efficiency. Thus began the era of "high-tech" locomotives with microprocessor (computerized) control of various locomotive functions (such as fan cooling) and even more horsepower being wrung out of each cylinder. The battle between reliability and fuel economy was the challenge of the 1980s.

The GE four-stroke cycle engine had an inherent advantage over the two-cycle EMD in fuel economy, and GE was quick to pounce on its superiority. By the mid-1980s GE and EMD were neck-and-neck in sales, and the lead would shift depending on who had gotten the latest order from the biggest railroad. By the 1990s GE was solidly in the lead as General Motors was vacillating in corporate indecision about what to do with its locomotive division. The main plant in LaGrange, Illinois, near Chicago, was downsized, and most of the final locomotive assembly was moved to the General Motors Diesel Division's much smaller factory in London, Ontario, Canada.

In the 1980s, the Canadian National Railway designed a "safety cab" for its hood units that would give the crews better crash protection and weather comfort. The design eliminated the short hood in favor of a heavily reinforced full-width nose. In 1989 both EMD and GE began offering similar cabs on their production units. The new "super cab" units soon grew to the 4,000-hp range over six motors.

AC: The Third Generation

Alternating current is much more efficient to generate than direct current, and AC traction motors are much more rugged than DC motors. But AC is much more difficult to control, since an AC motor always wants to synchronize with the rotating frequency of the generating source. This makes AC very difficult to handle in a locomotive, where speed ranges from zero on up with infinite variations in between. As a result, the earliest diesel-electrics used direct current for both the generator and traction motors.

Thanks to the development of a heavy-duty transistor diode in the 1960s, both GE and EMD began to offer AC/DC locomotives with efficient AC alternators feeding conventional DC traction motors. The GP40, SD40, and SD45 were all AC/DC units, as were their GE counterparts.

The ultimate goal, however, was a "pure" AC unit that could take advantage of both the efficient alternator and the virtually indestructible AC traction motors which worked strictly on induction and required no maintenance-prone commutators.

In the late 1980s, EMD teamed up with Siemens of Germany to apply their AC experience to the U.S. market, while GE drew on its own electrical expertise to develop an AC system. Both worked well, and soon AC traction was rewriting the textbook on the application of raw power to the rails. Since an AC motor will not overheat even

For most of the last half of the twentieth century, Electro-Motive's 3,000-hp SD40/SD40–2 served as the universal mainline freight locomotive for North American railroads. In May 1999 at "Brick Yard Curve" near Altoona, Pennsylvania, on the former Pennsylvania Railroad Philadelphia–Pittsburgh Main Line, a pair of Conrail SD40–2s assist an eastbound stack train coming down off the mountain from Gallitzin and Horseshoe Curve as an empty coal train tackles the eastbound climb. MIKE SCHAFER

ABOVE: Union Pacific DD35A No. 70 bullies its way into Evanston, Wyoming, as the conductor of an opposing freight picks up train orders in 1967. MIKE McBRIDE
BELOW RIGHT: Number 59, a 4,500-hp gas-turbine-electric, heads an eastbound freight at Ogden, Utah, in the 1950s. DON SIMS, RAILFAN & RAILROAD COLLECTION

Union Pacific = Unlimited Power

With its far-flung, high-speed main lines and awesome tonnage, the Union Pacific had become very much a motive-power-conscious railroad, always seeking bigger and faster locomotives. As a junior executive in the Motive Power Department in the early 1940s, David Neuhart was there when UP's top mechanical officer, Otto Jabelmann, unveiled his massive 4-8-8-4 Big Boy articulated steam locomotive and EMD was beating on the door with 5,400-hp FT sets.

The idea of using four diesel-electric units to replace one steam locomotive never sat well with Neuhart, and in 1949 when he became the railroad's top mechanical officer, he began a long program to prod the builders into developing bigger individual locomotives. His first success was with GE, which was already putting its wartime experience with jet engines to work in developing gas-turbine engines for commercial use. In 1952, GE delivered ten 4,500-hp gas-turbine locomotives to UP based on a 1948 experimental unit. Impressed, the UP soon ordered 15 more turbines.

But Neuhart and GE were working on something even bigger—a massive gas-turbine-electric that would deliver 8,500 hp! When these newest turbines were delivered in 1958, the new "World's Largest Locomotive" could be found running beside the "World's Largest Steam Locomotive" Big Boys. With a bit of "tweaking," the big turbines were soon cranking out an incredible 10,000 horsepower each!

But turbines, while incredibly powerful when working at full throttle, were almost as fuel hungry when idling and working at low speeds. Because of this, they were at their best only when they were kept moving on heavy loads and fast trains. Far too much of railroading does not fit that definition, unfortunately, even on the Union Pacific. The smaller but more versatile diesels were still the optimum overall locomotives.

By 1963 Neuhart had concluded that he needed 15,000 horsepower to effectively handle an average UP freight train. That came to six of the 2,500-hp units like the GE U25B. Since maintenance cost for a single locomotive was about the same regardless of horsepower, Neuhart figured that the more horsepower per unit, the lower would be his maintenance costs. He asked the builders to return to the twin-engine concept that had been proven so well over the years with Electro-Motive's passenger diesels to create twin-engined freight units in the 5,000-hp range.

GE was the first to bite, in essence placing the workings of two U25Bs on a single underframe with a high-set cab on one end. The resulting "U50" was a true monster in appearance, but in reality just a new combination of proven components. Meanwhile, Alco was wringing 2,750 hp out of its new 16-cylinder 251 engine and followed the same basic format as GE by placing two of them in one carbody to create the 5,500-hp Century 855.

EMD followed by taking the machinery of two of its new 2,500-hp GP35s and placing them on a frame over a pair of four-axle ("D") trucks to create the 5,000-hp DD35. EMD offered the DD35 as a booster only, preferring to use its off-the-shelf GP35 as a cab unit for the set.

Neuhart and the UP were impressed and ultimately acquired 23 GE U50s and 27 EMD DD35s, but only one three-unit A-B-A set of Alco C855s. In 1964, Neuhart returned to EMD for 15 more DD35s, this time equipped with cabs as "DD35A's." The only railroad other than the UP to purchase new-generation double-diesels was Southern Pacific.

But the double-diesel horsepower race was not yet over, and its most awesome manifestation was yet to come. In 1969 GE offered a completely redesigned U50 that, instead of riding on four trucks linked by span bolsters, sat on two heavy six-wheel, three-motor C trucks. The new U50C was a more compact and efficient package yielding the same performance as the earlier U50.

Meanwhile, EMD had turned to its new 645 diesel engine and AC/DC electrical system to create one of the most impressive freight diesel-electrics to rule the rails. Two 645 prime movers were mounted on a "biggest ever" 98-foot 5-inch underframe behind a "cowl" cab to produce the DDA40X, yielding 6,600 horsepower in a single locomotive. The year 1969 was the 100th anniversary of the driving of the Golden Spike at Promontory, Utah, on May 10, 1869, which completed the first transcontinental railroad, and the new DDA40X's were numbered in the 6900 series and dubbed "Centennials" in honor of the occasion.

The UP bought 48 of the Centennials, and Dave Neuhart retired from the UP in 1970 with the monster diesels of his dreams each racking up nearly 20,000 miles a month, almost twice the mileage of the rest of the fleet. In its first year, Centennial 6900 put on 220,000 revenue miles—that is one fifth of what the highest-mileage 4-8-8-4 had done in its entire 17-year career!

when stalled under load like a DC motor will, that power was available at all times and under any speed conditions.

On an AC locomotive, the diesel engine drives an alternator that produces AC current, but that AC is immediately converted to DC by a bridge rectifier. Since an AC motor needs a pulse wave to operate, a computer-controlled solid-state "chopper" circuit converts that smooth DC and feeds the motor with an artificial AC wave that perfectly matches the speed and load requirement. It was the computer that ultimately made possible the true AC power systems.

With the tremendous potential of AC traction systems, both EMD and GE began working on entirely new diesel engines that could push the six-motor unit to 6,000 hp. This time it was GE who went overseas to adopt a lusty new prime mover built by Deutz of Germany, while EMD abandoned its two-cycle format to create a new four-stroke cycle "265H" engine. Both the GE and EMD engines developed 6,000 hp from 16 cylinders with dual turbochargers. In general size, they aren't much bigger than the 1,350-hp EMC 567 of 1939!

At the dawn of the twenty-first century, the railroads are settling down to three basic freight locomotives. For the heaviest service are the 6,000-hp AC units, while conventional six-motor AC/DC units in the 4,000–4,400-hp range are replacing the 3,000-hp SD40 as the everyday workhorse. Scurrying around the yards, down branch lines, and on road locals are the non-turbocharged 2,000-hp four-motor units.

And the freight trains just keep on rolling.

The new face of railroading for the twenty-first century is the "super cab" that can accommodate the modern two-person crew, with a conductor's desk on the left side, while the engineer runs the locomotive from the right side seat. Kansas City Southern 2030, shown in August 2000 on a unit coal train, is a brand new 4,400-hp General Electric AC4400CW, equipped with AC traction motors. The locomotive is heading a Southwest Electric Power Company coal train en route from Wyoming's Powder River Basin to Welsh, Texas. The train is shown at Blanchard, Louisiana, as it curves off the KCS's Shreveport Subdivision and on to the Texas Subdivision in what amounts to a big U-turn in the little town. If you look closely, you will see the rear portion of this train crossing the road in the distance. TOM KLINE

The Union Pacific yard at Ogden, Utah, is the launching pad for the assault on the Wahsatch Mountains. Here in July 1969, a freight is preparing to head east behind the awesome might of a 10,000-hp gas-turbine-electric that is working with four diesel units of more than 3,000-hp each. Smaller diesels are used to assemble the heavy mainline trains in classification yards like this one where cars with a variety of origins and destinations are gathered into trains that carry them over the road in groups that are arranged for the most efficient delivery.

4 How a Freight Yard Works

L ooking at the vast network of railroads that spans the continent, the operations appear to be incomprehensibly complex. How do all those cars get to where they're going?

Like any other business, it takes a mountain of paperwork to run a railroad, and in the old days everything was done by hand by an army of clerks spread throughout the system. The telegraph had given way to the telephone for communication by the twentieth century,

The Denver & Rio Grande Western's East Yard in Grand Junction, Colorado, is at the fingertips of yardmaster Dick Rose in the hump tower. The panel in the foreground controls the switches and retarders on the hump tracks. Immediately behind him is the yard switcher shoving cars over the hump, with the classification tracks out of the view to the left. When this photo was taken in August 1996, the D&RGW had been merged into the Southern Pacific, and in another month they would both become the Union Pacific. TOM KLINE

more than 200 feet away, but it worked too well. Imagine all freight cars within 200 feet of a reader screaming out their data at the same time!)

The AEI tags made it possible to report the exact time and location of every car directly into the railroad's database computer. As each car was loaded or emptied, that information would be added to its file in the database to generate way-bills, train consists, switchlists, and billing reports through computer printers and fax machines.

The big railway systems were quick to utilize the AEI system as a customer-service tool by making the central database computer accessible by telephone. A customer could phone directly into the computer and receive any car's latest reader location hit in real time. By the turn of the twenty-first century, these systems were being configured to be accessed over the Internet, and the full potential of the system has yet to be explored.

SWITCHING MOVES

When it comes to the actual car movements, railroading is deceptively simple. A car can move in only two directions on any given piece of track, and all of railroading is just a matter of repeating a couple of elementary sorting movements in endless combination and repetition. There are essentially only four things a locomotive can do with a freight car: (1) push it or pull it from one end; (2) set it aside onto another track; (3) run around it to get onto the other end of it; and (4) physically turn it around to go in the other direction.

The push or pull is obvious on a single track, and while it is the most common of all movements, it is also the least flexible. Even the earliest tramways needed to develop a way of diverging from one track to another, to split from one track to two. Once they could do that, the possibilities became infinite.

The earliest switches were simply splits in the guideway that required a man to push each wheelset to one side or the other. Then came the "stub switch" where the approaching single track was shifted a few inches side to side to select the desired diverging track. Later, the outer rails were made continuous, and movable "points" on the closure rails would select the route. A mechanical lever on a "switchstand" alongside would be used to move the points or stub rails. The switchstand would usually provide a place on the lever for a heavy padlock to secure the switch in either position to prevent tampering. Each railroad would have a standard lock that would work with a single

TOP: The "ACI" Automatic Car Identification label, an early attempt to interface freight cars with a computer, was a colorful bar code that was read by an optical scanner. One is shown on a boxcar at Greenville, Mississippi, in 1971.

ABOVE: The ACI label has been replaced today by the "AEI" tag, an electronic transponder, shown below the frame of a CP Rail covered hopper.

and microwave transmissions and computers began to take hold in the 1970s. Today most railroad paperwork is computerized, although it still requires some human attention to enter the correct data for each load and movement.

Many systems have been tried to directly scan car identification and locations directly into the computer, but reliable technology for that did not arrive until the late 1980s when the optical "ACI" (Automatic Car Identification) system was replaced with the new "AEI" (Automatic Equipment Identification) system. The older ACI system used an optical scanner to read reflective tags on each car, but the tags were often obscured by dirt and easily damaged by scrapes and abrasions.

The AEI system, which was made mandatory on all interchange equipment in 1994, consists of a passive tag on each car that uses two antennas bracketing a microchip, all imbedded inside a small metal package that protects it from weather and external damage. A "reader" sends out a radar signal that is picked up by one antenna and triggers a response in the other antenna from the microchip that sends out the car's reporting marks and number to the reader's beam. The reader supplies all the energy to activate the response through the radar beam, and no power supply is needed for the tag on the car. The tag will respond to a reader up to 20 feet away. (A battery-powered "active" tag was developed that would respond

standard key, which was issued to all authorized employees. These switch locks and switch keys, however, would be different from one railroad to the next. It was mandatory that any mainline switch be locked when not being immediately used by a working crew.

These manual switchstands are still the most common types in use today, although in many cases, particularly at mainline junctions, some sort of mechanical, electrical, or compressed-air mechanism is used to operate them remotely. Regardless of the apparent complexity of a piece of trackwork, it would invariably boil down to a combination of simple switches and/or crossings or "diamonds" (a point where two tracks cross with no route options other than straight through on either track; the "diamond" nickname refers to the shape of the track intersection itself).

Using a single switch and a parallel track, a crew could rearrange the cars in its train into any

ABOVE: The most basic element in railroading is the track switch. This "turnout" at Gouldsboro, Pennsylvania, on the former Lackawanna has a "high stand" marker with a locking handle at ground level and a point guard on the opposite side to help guide the wheel flanges past the movable points. This switch is lined against the tank car that is sitting almost atop the "frog" where the closure rails cross.

RIGHT: A lot of work can be accomplished on a simple arrangement of yard tracks. This small yard at Rutland, Vermont, in 1973 is where the Green Mountain Railroad ended and interchanged with the Vermont Railway.

order by simply setting cars onto the siding and then picking them up again from a different position in the train. For instance, if a train had cars arranged Locomotive/B/C/A/D/E, and the crew wanted to get car A to the front of the "consist" (i.e., train makeup, pronounced KON-sist), they would pull up alongside the siding and cut off the train behind car A. Then they would pull cars B/C/A up past the switch and shove car A into the siding. Then they would pull cars B/C back out onto the main line, throw the switch and shove them back onto the D/E cars. With the B/C/D/E cars left on the main line, the locomotive would then uncouple and move beyond the switch again and back into the siding to pick up car A. It would then pull out with car A and shove it back onto the rest of the train on the main line, which would now be arranged Locomotive/A/B/C/D/E. All railroad "switching" is simply an endless repetition of this simple logic.

Using more than one switch and siding increases the number of moves that can be done at once and makes the work go quicker and more efficiently. For instance, think of a train as a deck of cards that has been shuffled, and the crew desires to get them into groups of hearts, clubs, spades, and diamonds, with each group in numerical order. Using four sidings, the crew would first assign a track to hold only the cars of one suite. They would grab as many cars as would be convenient to handle with the length of the switch lead and the power of the locomotive (usually around 20 cars or less, as longer "cuts" tend to become difficult to start and stop) and begin shoving the cars into the proper tracks to group all the hearts together, diamonds together, and so on. Once the train was broken into four tracks of similar suites, it would then pull out one track at a time and play put-and-take between the main line and siding to return the cars to the siding in the desired numerical order. All railroad yard switching is based upon this elementary logic.

If a locomotive needs to get to the other end of a freight car, it requires a "double-ended" siding with a switch at each end. The engine shoves the car into the siding and then runs down the main track to the other end and moves through the other switch and in against the opposite end of the car. If a double-ended siding is not available, a car can sometimes be rolled out of a slightly sloping siding by gravity using the handbrake. If that is not possible, the car can be "dropped" into the siding by uncoupling it from the moving locomo-tive and throwing the switch between them as the separated locomotive and car pass. This is a tricky maneuver, however, and requires skill and careful timing on the part of the crew. Even the smallest railroad yard will usually have at least one double-ended "run-around" track in it.

If a car (or more commonly, a locomotive) needs to be physically turned around, it must use a (1) balloon loop, (2) wye track, or (3) turntable. The balloon loop is the simplest but takes up the most physical space, since the track simply loops out and returns to the switch. A wye is a triangle-shaped pattern of track using three switches where the locomotive traverses one side, backs up on the first leg and pulls forward on the other leg, thus being turned around.

A turntable is a large bridge structure resting on a center pivot and its outer ends riding on a "ring rail." The bridge simply rotates on its center axis and is lined up with the approach track. Incredibly, with a locomotive properly balanced on a well-maintained and lubricated turntable, two people can fairly easily swing it around manually using long handles on the outer ends of the table itself. This is known as an "armstrong turntable," in reference to the human "arm" strength required to move it. The larger and more elaborate turntables are powered by a compressed air mechanism or electric motor. Steam locomotives generally operated better when running forward, making turntables desirable and necessary. Diesels, however, can work equally well in either direction and permitted the demolishing of most turntables.

A TYPICAL FREIGHT YARD

Before the Civil War, the Illinois Central had been chartered to build from the southern tip of its namesake state northward, with lines splitting at Centralia to reach both Dunleith (now East Dubuque, Illinois) on the Mississippi River and Chicago on Lake Michigan. By 1885 the railroad had expanded south all the way to New Orleans and west from Dubuque, Iowa, across the agricultural heartland of the "Hawkeye State" to Sioux City on the Missouri River. By this time, Chicago was rapidly growing into the economic center of the Midwest, and within five years the IC had built a direct line westward from Chicago to connect with the "charter line" at Freeport, Illinois. It also built a main line southwest from Fort Dodge, Iowa, to a connection with the Union Pacific's transcontinental railroad at Council Bluffs and Omaha.

The Chicago-to-New Orleans main line soon became the IC's most prosperous route, and the Centralia–Freeport charter line settled down to a secondary status serving the local agriculture. The Iowa lines continued to do a respectable business with a good hold on the agricultural and meatpacking traffic out of Fort Dodge and Cedar Rapids, as well as interchange off the UP, although in this case the IC was just one of six railroads competing for the Omaha–Chicago business.

Freeport, 116 miles west of Chicago, where the Chicago line and charter line met, became a "division point" with a freight yard and big roundhouse for servicing the steam locomotives. Business in the old downtown freight yard soon outgrew its capacity, and the newer Wallace Yard on the west side of town became the focal point of Freeport's activity. With the end of steam, the downtown roundhouse was demolished, and in the early 1960s its 100-foot turntable was moved to a new smaller diesel facility at Wallace.

In 1970, Wallace Yard was still a classic steam-era operation, essentially unchanged by the coming of the diesel. The railroad was using radios, but the labor agreements still required five-man crews and cabooses.

Crews based at Freeport (their "home terminal") worked the main line east to Chicago, turning

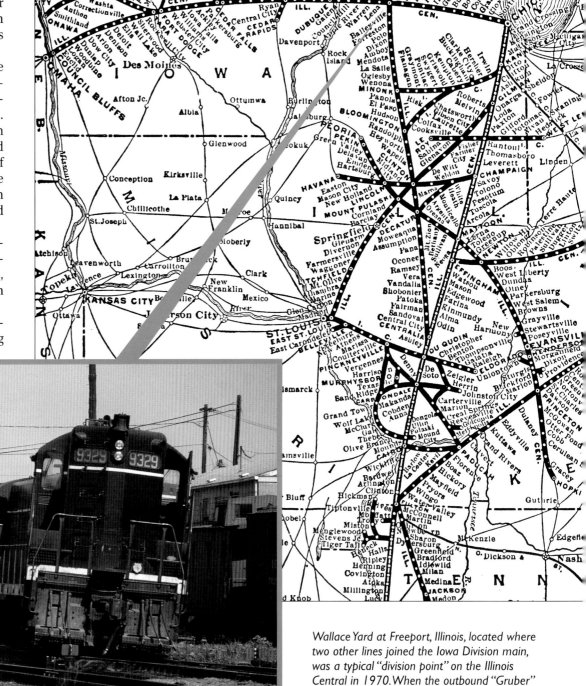

Wallace Yard at Freeport, Illinois, located where two other lines joined the Iowa Division main, was a typical "division point" on the Illinois Central in 1970. When the outbound "Gruber" local to Mendota got derailed in the crossovers in front of the yard office, it plugged up the Westbound Main and the East Yard, where two other freights were waiting to depart.

south at the lakefront to reach the huge Markham Yard on the New Orleans main line south of the city. Freeport crews also operated the charter line (known as the "Gruber") 164 miles south to Clinton, Illinois, as well as the Madison Branch, 64 miles north to Madison, Wisconsin. The Iowa Division main line west of Freeport was worked by crews out of Waterloo, Iowa, who would come into Wallace, lay over in a hotel for eight or more hours, and then take their assigned westbound trains back home to Waterloo.

In 1970, there were three scheduled through freights and an overnight passenger train, the *Hawkeye*, in each direction on the Chicago main line each day, along with a six-day-a-week local freight. The Gruber line south to Clinton had one daily through freight in each direction, as well as the "Mendota Turn" which would run 63 miles south to Mendota and then "turn around" and head back to Freeport, doing all local switching along the way except at Dixon, where a switch engine was kept on duty to handle extensive local business there. The Madison Branch was worked with a daytime local which would make a round trip every day except Sunday.

There were two switching locomotives assigned to Wallace to cover yard jobs that went to work at 7:59 A.M., 3:59 P.M., and 11:59 P.M., as well as an afternoon "Kelly Job" which would work Wallace and the downtown "city yard" as well as the Kelly-Springfield tire factory just east of town. The yardmaster's office and a couple of clerks were in the yard-office building, as well as the crew caller's office, trainmaster's office, and a crew lunchroom.

A typical freight yard is made up of a long "lead" track connecting to a "ladder" of switches to the various parallel tracks. Although some yards are stub-ended because of restricted available space, the most useful are double-ended yards with ladders at each end. Wherever possible, a yard will be graded to slope slightly downhill away from the ladder so that cars will not accidentally roll back into the ladder and lead where the crew might be working. On a double-ended yard, the tracks would be graded into a "bowl" so that any free-rolling cars would end up in the middle of a yard track.

Since everyone needs to be able to describe where they are working, every track on the railroad is given a name or a number. These are kept as simple as possible, but some have fascinatingly historic origins. The five tracks in front of the Wallace yard office in 1970, for instance, were (from

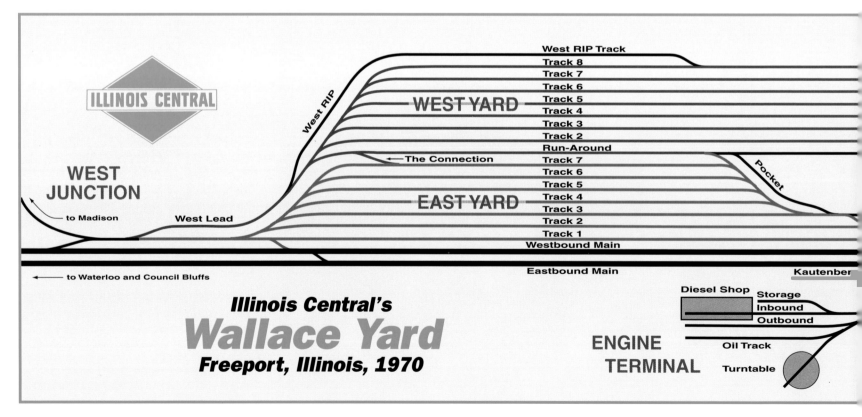

ILLINOIS CENTRAL

WEST RIP

WEST RIP Track
Track 8
Track 7
Track 6
Track 5
Track 4
Track 3
Track 2
Run-Around

WEST YARD

← The Connection
Track 7
Track 6
Track 5
Track 4
Track 3
Track 2
Track 1
Westbound Main

EAST YARD

Pocket

WEST JUNCTION

→ to Madison

West Lead

← to Waterloo and Council Bluffs

Eastbound Main

Kautenber

Diesel Shop
Storage
Inbound
Outbound

Illinois Central's
Wallace Yard
Freeport, Illinois, 1970

ENGINE TERMINAL

Oil Track

Turntable

The "Bullet," Illinois Central westbound freight CFS-3 (Chicago–Fort Dodge–Sioux City), got out of Chicago late each afternoon and is shown here in 1970 at 21st Street interlocking where the joint trackage with the Santa Fe crosses the passenger lines out of Union Station and Dearborn Station. CFS-3 was the "clean-up" job out of the huge Markham Yard and carried everything bound for northern Illinois and Iowa that was in the yard at the end of the day. While most Iowa trains out of Chicago were "pre-blocked" for western destinations, the Bullet would have its cars sorted out at Wallace Yard. Arriving at Wallace, CFS-3 would pull into Track 2 in the West Yard (BELOW) and would be the first thing worked by the Midnight Yard Job. By dawn, its cars would be ready to continue westward or be taken north to Madison or south down the Gruber or spotted at customers in Freeport.

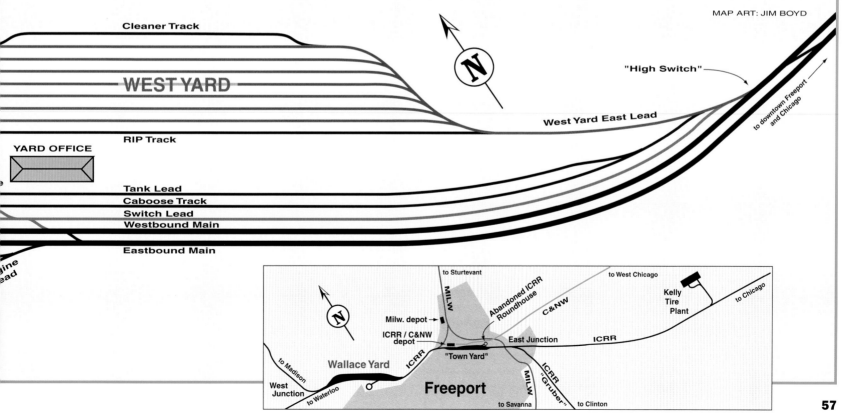

MAP ART: JIM BOYD

Cleaner Track

WEST YARD

"High Switch"

West Yard East Lead

to downtown Freeport and Chicago

RIP Track

YARD OFFICE

Tank Lead
Caboose Track
Switch Lead
Westbound Main

Eastbound Main

to Sturtevant   to West Chicago

MILW   Abandoned ICRR Roundhouse   C&NW   Kelly Tire Plant   to Chicago

Milw. depot

ICRR / C&NW depot   East Junction   ICRR

to Madison   ICRR   "Town Yard"

Wallace Yard   MILW   ICRR "Gruber"

West Junction   to Waterloo   Freeport   to Savanna   to Clinton

57

ILLINOIS TERMINAL RAILROAD COMPANY
SWITCH LIST
Form 432-10-A
Rev. 4/22/71

#1 N-5

TRAIN OR TRACK	CONDUCTOR	TIME	DATE
			5-28-77

	INITIALS	NUMBER	L/E KIND	FROM TO OR ROAD BEYOND	Tons	CONTENTS
1						
2						
3						
4						
5						
6						
7						
8						
9						
10	NW	500513		NW	XF	506
11	ITC	9287		4	load	
12		7431			XF	521
13	WAB	534				
14	HC	1500				
15	NW	208717		NW	2	
16	WAB	629			XF	521
17	CEI	196			XF	520
18	MTX	98706			XF	520
19	MP	818036				
20	ITC	1503				
21		1117				
22		1119			517	
23	TTHX	92393				
24		19796			514	
25	MC	215036			513	
26	NW	200310		NW 1		
27	HLX	14093			XF	512
28	TTHX	92406				
29		9275			XF	523
30	ATX	1041			XF	523
31	MTX	18208			XF	516
32	CEI	196285				516
33	PSPX	17061			XF	517
34	CEI	19747			XF	
35	ATX	96213			XF	535
36	ITC	1500				
37	NW	300431		NW tractor 506		
38	ACFX	53002		Brdho load		
39						
40	MTX	95283		XF Sideswiped		
41						
42						
43						
44						
45						
46						
47						
48						
49						
50						

Before the days of computer print-outs, all railroad switching and car accounting was done on hand-written documents. A crew would work from a switchlist like this one from the Illinois Terminal at Springfield, Illinois, in 1977. Each railroad would have its own system for abbreviating destinations. MIKE SCHAFER COLLECTION

south to north) the Eastbound Main, Westbound Main, Switch Lead, Caboose Track, and the Tank Lead (the steam-era water tank was long gone, but the name remained). When they were not coupled to their trains, all cabooses were gathered on the Caboose Track adjacent to a supply shed where a cleaning crew would keep them tidy and stocked with necessary safety and convenience supplies.

The first track behind the yard office was the RIP Track, which is a universal name for the repair track ("RIP" standing for Repair In Place) where minor "running repairs" are done on "bad-order" cars. This could be anything from changing brake shoes to fixing loose ladders or brake rigging or securing a damaged door or a shifted load. Cars sustaining heavy damage would be repaired to the point where they could be safely moved to a major shop for overhaul.

Wallace was actually two seven-track yards laying side-by-side. The yard adjacent to the double-track main line was the "East Yard" where eastbound Waterloo–Chicago trains and southbound Gruber trains were handled. The "West Yard" behind the yard office took care of westbound trains out of Chicago bound for Iowa points, the Madison Branch run, as well as inbound trains off the Gruber.

Why did they need a "classification"-type yard in Freeport, anyhow? Why not Rockford, 30 miles to the east, which generated five times the local industry traffic? Freeport itself had enough local industry to require the services of a switch engine and a small yard, but Freeport had developed as a "division point" where the steam locomotives were changed and serviced, because its distance from Chicago, 116 miles, was a typical "day's run" in the early steam era. It was also ideal for a classification yard because the Gruber line and Madison Branch converged there. The hundred-or-so cars a day that came north into Freeport off the Gruber had to be sorted between eastbound and westbound destinations, and the same applied to the Madison Branch trains, with a couple dozen cars a day. This traffic was much greater, of course, early in the 1900s, but the patterns remained essentially the same during our sample period of 1970.

The Midnight Switch Engine

No job typified the true character of Wallace Yard like the Midnight Switch Engine—technically the "11:59 P.M. Yard Job." In 1970 this required a four-man crew: the engineer, foreman, and two switchmen. In the steam era the train crews were separated between "yard men" and "road men." The yard men typically worked regular 8- to 12-hour shifts ("tricks" in railroad parlance) and never left town, while road crews would take mainline trains out to the next division point, where they would go off duty, lay over in a hostelry, and return the following day. A short branch line that could be worked in one day was usually handled by a road crew as a "turn" or "flip" job that would go out to a remote destination and then return to the same yard when the work was completed.

A yard job had a "foreman," while a road job had a conductor. Each was the boss of the crew and performed essentially the same job. The yard employed "switchmen," while the same job on the road crew was a "brakeman" or a "flagman." When he was hired and qualified for work, each railroader would establish his "seniority" date, which would be his permanent "rank" in the local workforce for his entire career. As the older men retired, each remaining man would move up, but they always remained in same seniority order relative to each other. On a railroad, typically one half to one third of the men had enough seniority to hold "regular" jobs with predictable workdays and hours. The rest of the men would work off the "Extra Board," where they would get called for the next open job as it came up. At Wallace, the extra men saw a lot of the Midnight Switch Engine and almost always worked one of the Gruber Clinton jobs. And since this was 1970, the IC out of Freeport was still a "man's world" that had no female train service employees.

The labor agreement required an hour-and-a-half warning "call" for any Extra Board job, and a man near the top of the Extra Board in the evening was always waiting for the phone to ring at 10:29 P.M. with a call for the Midnight Job. When he reported for duty, the foreman would assign the switchman's tasks as "pin puller" or "field man." The field man would line the switches and secure any handbrakes as needed in the classification tracks, while the pin puller worked the yard lead with the foreman, coupling and uncoupling the cars as they were switched.

Even though the yard tracks had the traditional center "bowl" to prevent roll-outs, Wallace was considered a "flat" yard. Since pushing and pulling each switching move with functioning air brakes would be impossibly time-consuming, Wallace was switched by "kicking" the cars from the lead into the classification tracks. To kick in a flat yard, the locomotive would tie onto 20 or so cars and pull them out onto the yard lead, where they could be individually "kicked" into the desired track. To kick a car, the locomotive would rapidly accelerate to a brisk walking speed, and the pin-puller would lift the "cut lever" to uncouple the car. The pin puller would then signal a stop, and the engine would quickly slow down while the car continued to roll into the desired track. The switchman would then signal a "kick sign," and the engine would urge against the cars again, repeating the procedure. A good crew could get a half dozen cars all rolling at once and throw the switches in between them without ever stopping or reversing the switch engine.

The free-rolling cars would drift down into their desired yard tracks where they would be gently stopped by gravity in the center of the "bowl." As more cars were added, however, each cut would have a tendency to roll, and a couple of handbrakes would be set to provide some resistance and act as a moving bumping post. Kicking was a careful blend of efficient switching moves and some distressingly violent impacts down in the yard if the cars were kicked with too much enthusiasm for the desired rolling distance. Over the years, much merchandise inside of boxcars was damaged by kick switching.

To be able to roll free for kicking, all air had to be bled from the brake systems of each car. The first task of the field man on the Midnight Job was to go over to track 2 in the West Yard and "bleed the Bullet." Waiting on Track 2 would be "symbol" freight CFS-3, known as the "Bullet," which had arrived in the previous hour or so from Chicago. This was a Chicago–Fort Dodge–Sioux City (hence the "CFS" symbol) through freight, which by 1970 was also known as the "clean-up" job out of Chicago's huge Markham Yard every afternoon with all the local cars and non-priority westbound traffic. It would be typically 80 to 120 cars of general freight destined for Freeport and points west, north, and south of there.

The switchman would go to the back of CFS-3's caboose, grab the dangling air hose, and then turn the angle cock to vent the trainline to be sure the brakes were all fully set in "emergency" mode. Then he would walk the entire length of the train,

pulling or pushing the "dump valve" lever to completely drain each car's brake reservoir so that the brakes would be in full release and the car would be completely "dead" and devoid of brake air. While he was working his way to the west end, the rest of the crew had run their switch engine through the first open track to the West Lead of the West Yard, ready to go to work on the Bullet.

But how do you sort out 120 mixed-up freight cars going in four or more different directions? In the old days, the foreman would have in his hand a switchlist, hand written by an overworked clerk from CFS-3's conductor's hand-written "wheel report" train list, which he had compiled en route at his caboose office desk from the waybills accompanying each car in his train. By 1970, the IC was using computer printouts.

Working off a switchlist required a good knowledge of the towns on the railroad on every line out of Freeport, but the IC had worked out a standard "station code" system for its entire railroad that made it easy for even a rookie to work off a switchlist. In the IC code, each line was given a letter designation—the Chicago–Iowa main was

Every track on a railroad has a name, which the local crews must learn and use. At Illinois Central's Wallace Yard in Freeport in 1970, the switcher is idling on the Tank Lead, while the caboose is in its proper place on the Caboose Track. The two ground-throw switchstands controlled the crossovers on the Switch Lead, with the Westbound and Eastbound Mains in the foreground.

IC's Madison Branch was a picturesque 62-mile line from Freeport north to the Wisconsin state capital. The line was served by a daily-except-Sunday local freight, shown in October 1970 ambling along below Monroe, Wisconsin. The refrigerator car is one of six such URTX reefers leased by Pauley Cheese of Monroe.

The modern hump yard is the ultimate facility for sorting freight cars. On October 20, 1981, the Chessie System opened its huge new Queensgate Yard in Cincinnati to combine the work from older yards on the B&O, C&O, and L&N. It handled about 1.1 million cars a year. This view shows the arrival and departure yards around the outside, with the main hump and classification "bowl" in the center. The dark patches on the tracks off the hump are the air-actuated retarders. CHESSIE SYSTEM

the "W" line, while the Gruber was the "A" line and the Madison Branch was the "R" line. The stations en route were assigned a milepost number, and they were printed on the switch lists as, for example, W87 (Rockford), A35 (Dixon), or R62 (Madison). To line up a westbound train in station order, you just had to keep all the numbers in sequence: W127 (Lena), W145 (Apple River), W153 (Scales Mound), and so on. Since anything west of the division point at Waterloo would be switched again there, any number above W276 (Waterloo) was regarded simply as a "High West" and sent as a mixed-up bunch to Waterloo for the next yard crew to deal with.

Getting to work on the Bullet, the switch engine would drag out about 20 cars, and the crew would begin to kick them from the lead down into the desired tracks. The foreman would assign dif-

ferent destinations to each track. "We'll put the High Wests in Track 3, the Apple Rivers in Track 4, the Madisons into Track 6," etc. Any cars for the Gruber or local Freeport industries would be "put to the Connection," which would place them on Track 7 of the East Yard to be switched later.

Every freight train is made up of only two types of cars, "shorts" and "throughs." A through car is one that goes to the next classification yard (in the case of westbounds out of Wallace, to Waterloo or beyond), while a short is any car that needs to be set off by the train before it reaches that next yard. Generally speaking, the throughs can be grouped in random order but usually all together in one "block" at the end of the train, next to the caboose. The shorts would then be lined up in the train in station order, with the first station's cars placed nearest the locomotive. Thus, as the train made its way across the railroad, the next cars to be set off would be directly behind the locomotive. Any cars to be picked up en route would be identified as shorts or throughs and coupled into their proper location in the train.

Back at Wallace, after sorting out all the cars from the inbound Bullet onto the yard tracks, the midnight crew would go to work building the two outbound trains in the West Yard, which were the westward continuation of the Bullet and the local for the Madison Branch. They would begin by gathering all the High Wests and coupling them onto CFS-3's caboose and shoving them back into Track 2. Then they would reach into each of the tracks containing the sorted cars and begin building blocks of shorts in station order against the High West throughs. One track in the West Yard would be used for storing clean tank cars for loading at Apple River, and the yardmaster would have included on the switchlist the numbers of the cars that the customer had called for. These cars would be picked up and put in their proper place near the front of CFS-3.

When the last cars were assembled and the train was in proper order, the switch engine would "gather up" the cars to test all the couplings to make sure the train was solid. Then they would shove it a few car lengths to the air box. Wallace had an electrically driven air compressor that piped trainline air to strategic points in the yard where hoses from the "air boxes" would be connected to the train in place of the locomotive.

Once the train was "set" to the air box, a car-department worker known as a "car knocker" would go to work coupling up all the air hoses and inspecting all the train's brakes and wheel bearings.

With the Bullet set to the air box, the Midnight Job would then reach into Track 6 and pull out all

A pair of Alco road-switchers has just arrived at the Great Northern yard in Superior, Wisconsin, on June 14, 1963, with a transfer run. Transfer freights operate between the yards of either the same railroad, if it has more than one within a district, or of different railroads in a terminal city. In this case, cars having arrived in Canada at the DW&P Superior yard that are destined for the GN have been gathered by the DW&P yard switcher and assembled into a transfer train.

A westbound freight from Kansas City has just arrived at Gulf, Mobile & Ohio's yard in Bloomington, Illinois, in 1972, and its trio of F-unit locomotives cut from the train prior to being moved to the engine facility nearby. This view illustrates a classic yard "ladder" track which feeds all the main tracks in the yard. GM&O's Chicago–St. Louis main line passes around the yard at left; a St. Louis-bound freight is holding on the main line while its head end makes a pick up and a set out in the yard. MIKE SCHAFER

the Madison Branch cars and then sort them back into that track in station order. Then they would grab the entire train (usually 12 to 20 cars) and couple onto the caboose. They would then shove the completed Madison train to the air box on Track 6. With the Madison Job and the Bullet ready to go, they would then head up to the yard office for a "lunch" break around 3:00 A.M. After lunch the Midnight Job would go to work in the East Yard making up the two Gruber trains that would depart shortly after dawn.

As dawn began to break, the midnight crew could look with considerable satisfaction at a nice, neat yard and four road trains all ready to depart. There was one last task, however, and that was to work WC-2, the "first meat train," when it showed up from Waterloo around 7 A.M. This Waterloo–Chicago train was the hottest thing on the railroad, carrying fresh meat out of Iowa in refrigerator cars

and piggyback trailers bound for markets in Chicago and farther east. Wallace usually had a few "hot" cars (requiring fast, expedited service) for interchange in Chicago that would be coupled onto WC-2 just ahead of the caboose. The midnight crew would get a warning when WC-2 was a few miles out and would gather up the outbound cars and ramble through the East Yard to the west end. The meat train would stay on the Eastbound Main track and pull its rear end up past the switches at the west end of the yard. Any cars on WC-2 that were to be taken off at Wallace would be next to the caboose for the Midnight crew to pluck off before placing the outbound cars ahead of the caboose. Urgently working the hind end of the first meat train as the sun was coming up was always a satisfyingly dramatic way to wrap up the work day.

When WC-2 departed Freeport to speed its perishable cargo to Chicago, the Midnight Job's

work was done. The morning yard job would take care of any clean-up work, such as spotting repair cars on the RIP Track or taking unbilled empty cars back to the Cleaning Track on the north side of West Yard, where a contract scavenger would remove any scrap packing material and sweep any dirt, rotting corn, or grain out of the cars, making them suitable for another customer to load. The cycle of trains in and trains out and the shuffling of cars would be repeated over and over again, day-in and day-out, rain or shine, winter and summer.

HUMP YARDS

Freight yards like Wallace were scattered all across the country in the days of steam and are still fairly numerous today. In many cases, however, because of changing traffic patterns caused by mergers and line abandonments, such division-point yards have diminished in number and usefulness, while division-point locations themselves have changed.

Any city or town with local industry or customers will require a yard of some size depending on how much traffic is generated. Some yards are big enough to support a resident switch engine and a crew or two, while others are worked by mainline locals that stop off in town, do the work, and then move on.

"Classification" is the sorting of large groups of cars in a yard to numerous destinations, often hundreds of miles away. As the number of small division-point yards dwindled, the size and importance of the huge classification yards in or near the big cities grew. These yards sort cars interchanged by numerous railroads to a great variety of outbound destinations.

A typical modern classification yard will usually be a "hump" yard, with an artificial hill built on the yard lead to provide a gravity slope to rapidly move the cars into the classification tracks. Whereas a switch engine can handle only about 20 cars kicking into a flat yard, powerful diesel "hump engines" can shove an entire road freight over the hump in one slow, steady move. The switches are all remote-controlled from the hump tower, and sets of air-operated "retarders" regulate the speed of the cars as they roll into the classification bowl. A retarder is simply a big set of rail-like clamps that squeeze against the wheels of the rolling cars to regulate their speed. Early retarders required a skilled operator to judge the speed and manually operate the air valves. In a modern yard the whole thing is controlled by a computer, as radar checks the car's speed and a scale inputs its weight to precisely control the retarders. Even the speed and direction of the wind is computed into the retarder operation.

A hump yard is usually comprised of three elements: (1) a flat receiving yard with long parallel tracks that can hold entire inbound trains, (2) the hump and classification bowl, and the (3) departure yard, which like the receiving yard can handle entire trains. A train will enter the receiving yard, where the locomotives will be cut off, and the train is inspected and "bled" of air. Then the hump engine would couple onto the rear and begin to shove the entire train onto the lead and up to the crest of the hump. At the top of the hump, a "pin puller" switchman will uncouple the cars in singles or groups according to instructions called out to him by radio or loudspeaker from the hump tower. As the cars roll over the hump, gravity takes over, and they quickly accelerate down the hill. The retarders go to work with an alternating "whoosh" and squeal as they set the rolling speed to drift the cars far enough into the yard to couple gently (if everything goes right) to the cars already there. The yard may be much bigger and more technologically complex than a yard like IC's Wallace, but the sorting logic is exactly the same.

When enough cars for a specific destination are gathered in the classification bowl, they are pulled out to the far end and assembled in the departure yard into outbound trains. Because of the efficiency of the hump yard and the capability of diesels to "just keep going" without the need to be changed out for maintenance or servicing en route like a steam locomotive, trains on the bigger railroads are often "blocked" for destinations thousands of miles away and even on different railroads.

No matter how big or automated a freight yard becomes, however, every move still comes down to the same "put-and-take" logic of two tracks and a switch. That is the secret of railroading.

One of the biggest hump yards in Chicago is the Belt Railway of Chicago's busy Clearing Yard on the south side of town, where major railroads from the east and west meet to interchange traffic. Clearing is interesting in that its yard tower is on a bridge over the crest of the double-track hump. Here in the early 1990s, a GP38 is nosing over the hump with one of the pneumatic car retarders in the foreground. The cylinders on the outside actuate rail-like pads which clamp down on the rims of the wheels to control their speed—which is measured by radar and calculated by a computer, that factors in the car's weight—to roll the car into the classification bowl at the right speed for a safe and gentle coupling. BRIAN SOLOMON

A classic American coal train, powered by an Electro-Motive GP30 and GP40, rolls westward on Baltimore & Ohio's Cumberland–St. Louis "West End" line, approaching Keyser, West Virginia, in October 1977. Although these cars are empty, returning to the mines, they are as important to the railroad's business as the loads, because the railroad must be able to keep a constant flow of empties available for the mines to load. Because coal cars are often gathered and sorted for delivery at a specific time, the B&O used the flat yard at Keyser as its "coal collecting yard," while the merchandise traffic was handled at the big hump yard at Cumberland, Maryland, 23 miles to the north.

5

King Coal

The "energy crisis" of the 1840s was a matter of coming up with a viable home-heating fuel as the virgin forests were being chopped back to supply the rapidly increasing number of fireplaces and stoves in the cities and towns. America was abundant with coal, but it was not usually deposited in convenient places. The earliest inland transportation systems—riverboats and canals— were often created to tap coal supplies. The first,

A view from the cab of a Burlington Northern Santa Fe SD70MAC locomotive at Gentry, Arkansas, reveals an engine crew's view of a coal train being unloaded at the Southwest Electric Power Company's Flint Generating Station. There is no crew in the cab, though, because the process is automated. TOM KLINE

the Delaware & Hudson Canal & Coal Company's gravity system in Pennsylvania, was also often focused on transporting coal.

The earliest coal cars were simply four-wheel flatcars with low wooden sides, and the coal was shoveled both in and out by hand. These later became known as "gondola" cars, and because of their simplicity, they continued to see service over the decades for a variety of loads. A gondola is basically a flat-bottomed car, even though some were equipped with drop-open doors in their floors for unloading.

Far more efficient for coal handling, however, were "hopper" cars with sloping floors and trap doors on the bottom. The earliest of these were four-wheel wooden "jimmies" that could be loaded from above from a chute and emptied through the bottom doors, usually over a small bridge or pit beneath the track. These elementary cars would carry about five tons of payload and were easy to move around on the loading tracks. Their flexibility permitted them to survive well into the 1880s, long after most other four-wheel cars had been forsaken in favor of those riding on a pair of four-wheel "trucks."

Nearly all the early hoppers were made of cheap and abundant wood. The design of railroad cars has always been a balance between cost and longevity, and each railroad tended to standardize its own design for efficiency of manufacture and maintenance.

One of the first railroads to explore the efficiencies of bigger hoppers made of iron was the Baltimore & Ohio, which began building them in the 1840s. The B&O cars were comprised of three cylindrical "pots" aligned side-by-side and riveted together, with each having a conical lower section tapering to a bottom door for unloading. The iron pots were bracketed by a wooden frame that supported the trucks and coupler draft gear. These unusual-looking cars ranged in capacity from eight to ten tons, roughly double that of the five-ton four-wheel jimmies.

Throughout the late nineteenth century, wood and iron hoppers worked side-by-side as the metal cars proved their superiority. As the nation's technology and manufacturing capacity grew, steel replaced iron as the favored material for railroad equipment and track construction. By World War I, the railroad industry had standardized on the steel two-bay 50-ton hopper, which was an optimum balance between capacity and weight for the steam era, as it spread its weight gently enough to negotiate often-crude mine siding

The Baltimore & Ohio was one of the nation's first "coal roads," and this view from about 1870 shows their distinctive iron "pot hoppers" rolling through Martinsburg, West Virginia, with a Davis Camel 4-6-0 steaming off to the right. The Berkeley Hotel was built in 1840s and survives today essentially unchanged, with the Amtrak and Maryland MARC commuter passenger station at track level. HERBERT H. HARWOOD JR. COLLECTION

trackage and still carry a useful load. One interesting throwback occurred during World War II when a shortage of steel brought the return of the wooden hopper in the form of "composite" cars with steel frames and bracing and wooden sides.

As the track improved in the mid-twentieth century, hoppers grew in capacity and size to three and four bays and up to 70 tons. By the 1960s, railroads were upgrading their track as new 100-ton capacity roller-bearing trucks permitted the cars to grow even more. Lightweight construction and carbody materials permitted a reduction in the dead weight of the car and a relative increase in load capacity while maintaining an acceptable axle loading.

FLOOD LOADING AND FAST DUMPING

With their open tops, hoppers have always been easy to load from simple lineside chutes. The hopper, with its trap-door bottom, was much easier to unload than a flat-bottom gondola.

Hundreds of local coal dealers had simple wooden trestles where hoppers could be spotted and easily unloaded. But by the early twentieth century, the labor-intensive task of unlatching the doors to empty the car was already becoming a nuisance at power plants and export piers where hundreds of cars a day had to be handled. It would be much easier to simply pick up the car and turn it over to empty it. In a flourish of industrial enthusiasm, huge steam or electrically powered mechanical car dumpers were built that would either lift up the car and turn it on its side or simply rotate it upside-down on its own axis. These dumpers required each car to be spotted precisely in place and uncoupled from any adjacent car. Then huge clamps would drop down to hold the car on the rotating track as it was overturned. When the empty car was uprighted, it was pushed out of the dumper by the next incoming car, and the process would be repeated.

Most of the large dumpers were built with spectacular "kick-back" tracks, where the empty cars would drop down a steep ramp and pass through a spring-loaded switch onto a sharply inclined uphill ramp. Gravity would quickly stop the car and cause

ABOVE: Although it came in many shapes, the 50-ton hopper was the standard of the steam era, primarily because that was the load limit on the trucks (wheel assemblies) of the day. Here in 1956, Norfolk & Western Y6-b 2179, a very modern compound 2-8-8-2, drifts downhill out of Bluefield, West Virginia, with one of the typical 100-car coal trains bound for "tidewater" at the Norfolk piers. The Bluefield yard lies north of the main line, and here at RD tower the trains cross over to the right-hand eastbound main for the run to Roanoke. ALVIN SCHULTZE

ABOVE LEFT: Roller bearings, heavier truck sideframes, and larger wheels permitted the 100-ton cars that are typical today. Denver & Rio Grande Western 16606 is essentially a 100-ton version of the steam-era 50-tonner, with four bays and conventional bottom doors. It is on an eastbound coal train at Phippsburg, Colorado, in June 1977.

it to roll back toward the dumper, but the spring switch would direct it onto a track around the dumper and into an empty-car holding yard.

In the 1960s, rotary-shank tightlock couplers were developed so that standard-sized cars could be unloaded in a specially designed dumper that rotated the car on the axis of the couplers. In this manner, the cars did not need to be uncoupled in order to be overturned for dumping. And with the rotary coupler came the return of the high-side gondola for coal transport. A gondola typically has no bottom doors, and by eliminating the structure of the hopper bays and door mechanisms, the cars could be constructed with less overall weight and more payload for the same overall size. "Bathtub" gons with rounded belly troughs between the trucks further increased payload capacity while staying within the standard dumper dimensions.

ABOVE: A classic small-town lumber yard and retail coal dealer stands alongside the N&W's former-Virginian Railway yard in Oak Hill, West Virginia, in 1973. Note the bales of lumber and the hopper on the coal trestle. These small bridge-like structures were once a common part of the American landscape.

RIGHT: The Wheeling & Lake Erie had this rotary dumper at Huron, Ohio, on Lake Erie. The hopper in the foreground has been rolled into position and stopped by the brakeman riding the handbrake. The "barney" is a cable-powered pusher that rides rails in a trough between the running rails. It is shown at the top, behind the hopper it has just placed at the dumper, and will come back down the ramp, duck under the standing car and rise up behind to shove it to the top. Since the car dumper is in a fixed position on the pier, the boat will move fore and aft to position the chute for loading in the proper cargo holds. Out of view on the other side of the channel from the Louis W. Hill is a set of Hulett unloaders that empty the boats that arrive with iron ore and then depart from the coal pier loaded with outbound coal.
RAILFAN & RAILROAD *MAGAZINE COLLECTION*

Since two rotary-shank couplers together would be inherently unstable, each car would have a rotary coupler on one end only, with a standard tightlock coupler on the other end. To assure that the train would be lined up correctly before being unloaded, the end with the rotary coupler was always painted with a bright contrasting color, giving these "unit trains" a distinctive appearance.

From the beginning of railroading, the customer was billed by the weight of his transported commodity. In the case of coal, special tracks with large but precise balance scales were used to measure the weight of each car empty and loaded. At the mine, a car would be weighed and recorded on its waybill (the sheet of paper which follows the car and tells what it contains, where it originated, and where it is destined, as well as the customer who is paying the bill). The car would often be weighed again before it was unloaded. Customers would generally tolerate a 5 percent loss in transit due to leakage or spillage without complaint as a normal part of business. The weight of the coal would also change substantially if it was exposed to rain or snow—and if the car was exposed to freezing rain, the coal would become one huge crunchy black ice cube that was nearly impossible to unload. In many locations, immense "thawing sheds" were constructed with radiant heaters to unfreeze the coal for unloading.

ABOVE: The functioning heart of a rotary coal dumper is the huge rotating drum that holds the hopper car. The hopper is positioned in the drum by the barney (note the cable pulley in the middle of the foreground track), and huge clamps are lowered across its top siderails to keep the car securely on the rails. The drum then rotates, dumping the entire load of coal in one move. After it rotates back into alignment with the track, the clamps are released, and the next car being pushed up the ramp bumps it out of the way. RAILFAN & RAILROAD *COLLECTION*

LEFT: The Chesapeake & Ohio Coal Pier 15 at Newport News, Virginia, in April 1983 shows the kickback track where empty cars are shoved out of the rotary dumper to roll downhill, through a track switch, and on to the ramp. They reverse direction and roll back clear of the dumper into the empty-car storage yard.

RIGHT: Rotary car dumpers made possible the modern high-capacity "bathtub gondola" cars used on unit coal trains. The "tub" beneath the frame simplifies construction and reduces the car's empty weight by eliminating hopper doors. The white panel indicates the end of the car that is equipped with the rotating-shank coupler that makes possible dumping without uncoupling the cars. Unit trains always match a rotating coupler with a fixed-shank coupler. This Chicago & North Western train is crossing the Illinois River on terminal railroad Peoria & Pekin Union at Peoria, Illinois, in 1980.

Weighing the loaded cars is a time-consuming process, but in the 1960s the railroads began to market the "unit train" concept for large shippers, where entire trainloads would originate at one point and be delivered to a single destination, with no intermediate switching or handling, and the entire 120-car train was carried on one way-bill. Supporting this marketing concept was the development of "flood loading" which filled each standard-sized car to full visible capacity (often with a "plow" swept over the top to guarantee the size of the load). This almost eliminated the need to weigh each individual car, as the time and expense of weighing was offset by the economy of not having to do it. For cars that still needed to be weighed, however, modern "weigh-in-motion" scales could handle an entire train passing over it at a steady 5 MPH.

DIFFERENT TYPES OF COAL

Coal is not a generic commodity. In addition to the two basic types of coal—hard, rock-like anthracite and soft bituminous—each seam produces coal with slightly different chemical content. Although we generally think of coal as a fuel to be burned in home furnaces, power plants, and even locomotive fireboxes, an equally important use for coal is as a source of chemical carbon in the making of making steel and other products, like paint pigments.

Thus coal is classified into two general types: "steam coal" that is burned as fuel, and "metallurgical coal" that is used for its chemical content. It is steam coal that fuels the huge power plants, while "met" coal goes to steel mills.

Coal for the steel process is often converted to coke before it is fed into the blast furnaces. The

This modern fast-loader is located on the Denver & Rio Grande Western at Energy, Colorado, on the branch up to Craig. In June 1977, a five-unit set of SD40T–2 diesels was easing the train through the tunnel beneath the coal pile, which contains the loading chutes in its center. This train will make its run to a power plant in Texas without ever having its cars uncoupled or broken up. Only the diesels will change when the train goes from one railroad to another.

Appalachia would glow at night with the light of Hades as row upon row of beehive ovens burned on the hillsides, spewing flames from their tops and spreading light from their ventilation ports.

By the mid-twentieth century, however, most steel companies had built their own industrial coking plants near their mills, and the rural coke ovens began to disappear. One of the last of the old beehive complexes, which operated into the late 1970s, was in Vansant, Virginia, and it was a horrifying and yet awe-inspiring sight at night.

MINES, LOADERS, AND PREP PLANTS

Regardless of whether it is steam or met coal, the raw product must be dug out of the ground, cleaned, graded, sized, and prepared for loading and transport. "Coal mine" is a generic term that applies to all combinations of these elements. As for the digging from the ground, there are four general types of mines: a drift mine, a slope mine, a deep shaft mine, and a strip mine (now called a "surface mine" in politically correct terminology).

Coal is a sedimentary rock created by water and decaying plant and animal material. When it was initially created, all coal was in horizontal

"coking" process involves burning the raw coal in an oxygen-deficient oven that removes the impurities but leaves almost pure unburned carbon. Into the early twentieth century this was done in "beehive" ovens made of brick and shaped like an Eskimo igloo. It was often desirable to produce the coke near the coal mines, and the hollows of

beds determined by the water. Over the ages the carbon matter was compressed and sometimes tilted by upheavals and folding of the rock.

A strip mine is used to gather coal from seams near the surface, where the "overburden" of rock and dirt is shallow enough to be economical to simply dig off and move out of the way. The early strip miners left terrible scars on the land, as they left behind barren bedrock and mountains of overturned and useless rocky soil that was incapable of sustaining renewed plant life. By the mid-twentieth century, new environmental laws mandated returning the stripped area to a reasonable semblance of its former appearance, with the topsoil returned to the surface area. Advances in the size of monster electric shovels and heavy mobile grading machinery returned the economy

to strip mining, as the surface restoration costs were kept in line. To this day, "strip mining" has a bad name, while "surface mining" implies today's environmental sensitivity.

A drift mine is a simple horizontal shaft that follows a coal seam exposed on a hillside, while a slope mine is essentially the same thing on a sloping coal seam that breaks the surface. Deep mines have vertical shafts that penetrate downward to reach seams that do not breach the surface.

Coal gets to know railroad cars very quickly, as narrow-gauge tramways with low-slung cars were until recently the most common method of moving the raw coal from the mining face to the surface. Today, conveyors are the preferred method, although tram-car operations are still quite numerous.

There's all sorts of activity going on at this typical Appalachian bituminous coal mine on the Baltimore & Ohio just north of Garrett, Pennsylvania, in 1967. Screens inside the tipple are used to sort the coal by size, and the different tracks are usually used to load different sizes of coal. This tipple is interesting in that it has three fairly short tracks beneath the tipple (and one outside storage track), whereas many loaders have much longer storage tracks, and the cars move beneath the structure for loading and are then rolled out of the way.

The Dora Mine on the Pittsburgh & Shawmut is a modern "prep plant" and loader where the coal is graded, washed, and sized for loading. Here on September 15, 1988, Dora is flood-loading a fleet of "local service" 55-ton steam-era hoppers to run only 21 miles west to the West Penn Power plant at Reesdale. Coal bound for interchange to other railroads off the P&S was loaded into modern 70-ton or 100-ton cars. The P&S replaced its steam locomotives in 1953 with these same EMD SW9 switchers.

With its diesels cut in between the empties for the Blue Diamond and Open Fork No. 2 tipples, the Clinchfield Railroad's Nora Branch job out of Dante, Virginia, is shoving caboose-first up the hollow past the Open Fork No. 1 loader in August 1974. In this narrow valley, a long single siding serves the loader.

Raw coal is not a particularly useful product as it comes out of the ground, and it needs to be run through a "preparation plant" to render it commercially viable. Here, the raw coal would be washed and sorted to remove slate and rock and then run through a series of sizing screens and crushers to reduce the huge chunks to the size and quality desired by the customer.

Most prep plants would have a number of loading tracks where coal of different grades and sizes could be loaded simultaneously. Sometimes all tracks would load the same type of coal, and sometimes the differences in product would be strikingly noticeable. Nearly all prep plants would have a yard on one side to hold empty cars and a yard on the other to hold loaded cars. Generally there would be a gentle downhill slope from the empty yard, through the tipple loading tracks and out into the load yard. A weighing scale was often placed between the tipple and the load yard so the car could be weighed immediately.

Not all coal loaders are tipples or prep plants, however. Many small mines produce only one or two carloads per day, and an elaborate prep plant would be uneconomical. These small operations would often just dump the "run-of-mine" coal into a hopper and move it by rail to a preparation plant elsewhere. That is why it is not unusual to see coal being delivered to a prep plant.

As the coal regions were developed, railroad branch lines would be snaked into every hollow where a coal mine was located, and even small mines were served directly. By the mid-twentieth century, however, trucks were growing in size and reliability, and many of the smaller operations turned to dump trucks to move the coal to a rail loader. It was often difficult to tell by appearances which coal loaders were productive and which were nearing the end of their economic life. While the massive new prep plants were obviously thriving, many simple truck-dump loaders were often responsible for keeping them humming!

TIPPLE TO TIDEWATER

Readers need to understand the aforementioned basics of the coal business to appreciate why the railroad's part in moving coal trains is not as simple as it might appear to be. In the mountainous regions of Appalachia, great carriers like the Baltimore & Ohio, Western Maryland, Chesapeake & Ohio, Norfolk & Western, and the Virginian Railway built their reputations by hauling coal with networks of branch lines reaching deep into the hills and hollows.

Bituminous out of Appalachia was useful as both steam and met coal, depending on the particular seam and mine. Steam coal was shipped nearly everywhere for use as heating fuel and for power plants. Met coal was usually destined for the steel mills of Pennsylvania, Ohio, and northern Indiana. Because of historic tariff agreements, it was sometimes desirable for power plants and steel mills located along the Great Lakes or major rivers to take delivery of their coal from barges and boats, rather than by rail. As a result, much steam and met coal was dispatched out of Appalachia toward an Ohio port on Lake Erie such as Ashtabula, Cleveland, Lorain, or Norwalk. As a result, any generally westward movement out of Appalachia was referred to as "lake coal."

The same pattern applied to many domestic destinations on the Atlantic seaboard. The other huge market for coal was export to Europe and beyond. Extensive coal ports were concentrated around the harbor at Norfolk, Virginia, and Baltimore, Maryland. Since it is affected by the rising and falling tides, an ocean seaport is referred to as "tidewater," and coal bound for an Atlantic seaport is called "tide coal."

A visit to the Chesapeake & Ohio in May 1975 provides an excellent example of the way coal is gathered and dispatched out of West Virginia.

Deep in the hills south of Charleston is the C&O yard at Danville, where a pair of weathered and worn GP7s heads south along the Big Coal River on a coal-collecting job known as the "Barrett Shifter." With empty hoppers in tow, it swings east along the Pond Fork and follows the river deeper into the hills. Near Barrett, it backs its train over a picturesque bridge and shoves caboose-first up to the Wharton No. 2 Mine where it drops off its empty cars in the yard above the tipple. A remote-controlled red diesel switcher will move the cars through the tipple on the proper tracks at the proper time.

The Geeps place their bright yellow caboose behind a cut of loaded cars and then gather all the outbound cars from the load yard, coupling them together into one train. Then they head down the mine spur and return to the Pond Fork line to go back to Danville. They repeat the pick-up procedure at the big Pond Fork tipple, as their train grows in length. At the tiny community of Van, they pause at West Junction to get clearance by telephone from the dispatcher to enter the line that comes in from the Cabin Creek branch to the east. As the Geeps idle in the afternoon sun, a group of local school kids splash happily alongside in the waters of Pond Fork.

Continuing homeward toward Danville, they pass a weed-grown spur near Brounland where the little Kanawha Central will occasionally leave a load or two from the rustic old loader five miles away at Olcott that is supplied by "coal bucket" dump trucks from a nearby mine. The Olcott

In August 1975, a pair of C&O GP7s are handling the "Barrett Shifter" on the Big Coal River line at the Wharton No. 2 tipple at Barrett, West Virginia. The crew has spotted their empties above the tipple, where they can roll downhill through the facility for loading, and are about to gather the outbound loads to take down the valley to the coal collecting yard at Danville. Thus begins a typical journey "from tipple to tidewater."

After departing Wharton No. 2 and returning to the Pond Fork branch August 1974, the Barrett Shifter in rolls past the Pond Fork Mine near Van, West Virginia. The coal business varies wildly from week to week and day to day depending upon ocean-going ship arrivals and specific coal contracts. Although Wharton No. 2 was busy, Pond Fork is not loading on this particular day.

A few miles down the Big Coal valley from Van is the five-mile-long Kanawha Central Railroad, which takes a few loads a day from the truck-dump loader at Olcott to the C&O interchange at Brounland with its sole locomotive, a tiny four-wheel Whitcomb diesel. This is about as short as a freight train can get.

loader is a simple affair that boasts two tracks, however, for simultaneous loading of different sizes of coal. The Kanawha Central's tiny four-wheel Whitcomb diesel is kept in a weather-beaten wooden enginehouse and will venture out whenever needed to lug a car or two down to the C&O interchange on the Big Coal. (By the way, "Kanawha" is pronounced locally "ka-NAW.")

In the Danville yard, the cars brought in by the Barrett Shifter are sorted out according to their intended destination, with the lake coal (westbounds) separated from the tide coal (eastbounds). Cars destined for a specific shipment at the port of Newport News will be assigned a movement code, like "Tide 614." All cars bound for that particular customer's shipment from Massey Pier No. 9 will be assigned that number, regardless of the tipple from which it had originated.

During the next few hours in Danville, the eastbound cars, including a dozen Tide 614s from Wharton No. 2 bound for Newport News, are weighed and gathered into a train of about 140 cars. Before dawn, three road diesels couple on and depart Danville for the main line at St. Albans, West Virginia, where they turn east and ramble up the Kanawha River valley through Charleston and the old division point yard at Handley to the New

River Gorge, a spectacular 60-mile valley with steep bluffs on either side. At Hinton, at the south end of the gorge, the train gets a set of pusher diesels for the climb over Allegheny Mountain, cresting in Big Bend Tunnel, which gained fame in the legend of Jawn Henry, "the steel-drivin' man" who worked himself to death in a race with a steam drill making holes for the dynamite used in blasting out the rock bore.

The coal train then drops down the mountain through White Sulphur Springs to Clifton Forge, Virginia, where it enters the yard. Over the past few days the C&O has been gathering other cars for Tide 614, and there are 58 more waiting at Clifton Forge to be cut into the train. The ship that will carry this load will be at Pier 9 in two days, and Tide 614 is beginning its final movement. The train is soon on its way again, moving easily down the C&O's magnificent double-track main line along-side the scenic James River, passing through Richmond on the final leg of its run to Newport News.

In many cases, a customer will want a specific blend of coal, made up of chemical properties from a number of different grades from a variety of sources. This is done in the "mixing bowl" yards like Newport News. The most practical way to mix a boatload of coal is to do it when loading and unloading, so a list is made up of specific cars in a specific order that are to be loaded into the hold of the ship. For instance, the customer might want a mix of one part A, two parts B and two parts C, and the yard contains a track of A cars, a track of B cars and a track of C cars (all, for example, identified as Tide 614, but each waybill describing the specific grade or source of the individual car's

coal). The switch engine will then line up its "train" for the dumper with cars in the repeating pattern of B/C/A/B/C, which will mix the coal in 70-ton increments in 350-ton batches in the ship's hold. The unloading process will mix the batches even further.

Newport News uses huge rotary dumpers to load the ship, with the cars shoved one at a time up to the dumper by a mechanical "mule" between the rails. Because of this mixing process of different grades of coal from different mines, Tide 614 is a traditional coal movement using conventional hopper cars that are weighed en route and go singly through the dumper.

BELOW: *During the day, road diesels idle at Danville in August 1974, while the various shifters gather the coal from the branches. During the night, they will move out with heavy mainline coal trains bound for either the Great Lakes or tidewater at Newport News.* MIKE SCHAFER

BOTTOM: *C&O diesel-powered tugboats were working the harbor at Newport News in April 1983 as two huge ocean-going coal carriers were tied up at the modern conveyor-equipped piers, while the older rotary dumper piers remained in place but unused.*

A modern-day coal train out of the Wyoming coal fields meets a more-traditional freight train on Crawford Hill, Nebraska, on Burlington Northern's main line between Billings, Montana, and Lincoln, Nebraska. The date is May 29, 1995, and in just four months, the BN will merge with the Santa Fe to form the Burlington Northern Santa Fe system. But the coal trains will keep rolling. *BRIAN SOLOMON*

UNIT TRAINS

Unit coal trains are rarely if ever used for the type of service where the cars are gathered from many sources and assembled along the route, only to be switched into a different order for dumping. The economy and efficiency of the unit train come from its being loaded with one grade of coal at one mine and moved as a "unit" to its single destination, with no switching or reordering of the cars en route.

To do this, the customer must find a source of coal that is satisfactory for his use without the mixing-bowl blending. Environmental laws on smoke pollution in the mid-twentieth century drastically reshaped the coal industry and the way that the railroads had to respond to it. Although the rich bituminous of Appalachia was superb coal, it was often excessively high in sulphur content, making it undesirable as steam coal, though it could still be used as met coal where the burning process was much more closely controlled.

In the twenty-first century, America's "coal country" is no longer Appalachia, but the windswept high plains of Wyoming, which is underlaid with expansive seams of low-sulphur coal that was previously too remote to be economical to develop for anything other than local business. With the advent of the huge new shovels to strip the overburden and unit coal trains to transport it almost anywhere in the country, the Wyoming coal was suddenly the most valuable and accessible in the world. The Burlington Northern, Union Pacific, and Chicago & North Western teamed up to build hundreds of miles of brand-new railroad into Wyoming's Powder River Basin in the 1970s as new mines and "fast loaders" sprang up all over the landscape. Suddenly coal mines were bearing Western names like "Black Thunder" and "Eagle Butte" instead of "Slab Fork No. 2" and "Pond Creek." The Powder River Basin supplies low-sulphur steam coal to power plants all over the country, and the lines radiating south and eastward from it are among the nation's most densely traveled freight routes.

"CARRYING COALS TO NEWCASTLE (ILLINOIS)"

Since the mid-nineteenth century, the phrase "carrying the coals to Newcastle" implied an illogical and senseless venture, since Newcastle was England's coal-mining heartland. But that is precisely what happened in the 1980s with the environmental pollution laws. Southern Illinois had

large beds of low-grade bituminous coal that was cheap and nearby for power plants all across the Midwest. The Chicago & Illinois Midland made a prosperous living in the steam era by hauling that coal northward to the Illinois River barge port at Havana (where it was shipped by water to Chicago) and the huge Powerton Generating Station south of Peoria. The big, high-side C&IM gondolas riding on six-wheel trucks were among the first truly high-capacity coal cars to see service in America, and they were a common sight at Midwestern power plants, large and small.

But southern Illinois coal is excessively high in sulphur content and soon became unusable even in plants equipped with "scrubbers" to clean the exhaust gases. Powerton, in particular, needed a new source of coal, and it came in the form of unit trains out of the Powder River Basin. In the 1980s,

traffic completely reversed on the C&IM, as the low-sulphur coal arrived at Peoria off the BN and C&NW and was handled south to Powerton by C&IM diesels. "Coals to Newcastle," indeed.

BARGING IN

The heart of the Kanawha River coal region just east of Charleston, West Virginia, was once laced with branch lines and shortline railroads reaching out of the valley into every hollow. One such hollow not only supported a half dozen substantial coal mines, but two competing shortline railroads that literally crossed all over each other to reach the rival coal companies. Unable to agree even on the spelling of their names, the Kelly's Creek Railroad and the Kelley's Creek & Northwestern both connected with the New York Central at Cedar Grove, on the north bank of the river,

The huge coal-fired power plant at Powerton, Illinois, just south of Peoria and Pekin was built to receive coal from nearby central Illinois mines on the Chicago & Illinois Midland. Environmental standards, however, made the high-sulphur Illinois coal unsuitable, and now coal is brought in from Wyoming's Powder River Basin. In July 1986, a set of C&IM diesels has just brought a Burlington Northern coal train into Powerton from Creve Coeur, where BN handed the train over to the C&IM. MIKE SCHAFER

The Kelley's Creek & Northwestern is the sole survivor of the two shortline railroads that criss-crossed each other up the valley of Kelly's Creek north of Cedar Grove, West Virginia. In July 1969, one of the KC&NW's GE 70-ton diesels works one of the coal loaders. The coal would go out over the Penn Central's former New York Central line into Ohio or by barge on the Kanawha River.

and reached inland about six miles along Kelly's Creek (the correct spelling).

Although they could interchange with the NYC and depend on the large carrier for a supply of empty hopper cars, they also made extensive use of simple barge-loading facilities on the Kanawha River at Cedar Grove, where small tug "work boats" would spot and gather the barges for movement about 60 miles northwestward down the Kanawha to the Ohio River near Point Pleasant, West Virginia. There, the barges would be gathered into large groups called "tows" that would be moved up or down the Ohio by large towboats to power plants, steel mills, and other customers in places like Cincinnati or Pittsburgh.

By the 1970s, the Kelly's Creek Railroad had been abandoned, and the KC&NW had expanded to take up all of the business remaining in the hollow. Since the railroad was all downhill from the mines to the river, small General Electric 70-ton diesels could handle the loaded coal trains down to the NYC interchange at Cedar Grove or to the barge loader. The cars would be dumped through their hopper bays onto a conveyor that would carry it out to the nearby river barge. There was just enough of an upward incline in the shed to let the empty car roll back by gravity out onto the "empty" storage track.

A few miles west, down the Kanawha on the south bank of the river, the little Winifrede Railroad

reached seven miles inland along Fields Creek to a big Carbon Fuel Company prep plant in South Hollow from a barge loader on the river. The dumper at Winifrede Junction, however, was parallel to the river and a modest-sized railroad yard alongside. To access the yard, the Winifrede exited the mouth of the hollow and ducked beneath the double-track Chesapeake & Ohio main line. At the east end of the yard was an interchange with the C&O, which also made use of the Carbon Fuel Company's "Winifrede Dock."

This interface between rail and water is much more common than most people would suspect, and it ranges in scale from small river barges and one-car loaders to huge tidewater yards and ocean-going ships.

CAPTIVE COAL RAILROADS

The cost-effectiveness of rail versus trucks was carefully calculated, and some interesting operations have developed. Coal mining is an inherently mobile business, as coal seams are mined and depleted, the operations and loading points can change over the years. Railroads are relatively expensive to build, but where the business in concentrated, rail still has a substantial economic advantage even in a very short haul.

In the 1940s, the Midland Electric Coal Company had a surface mine at Middle Grove, Illinois, just west of Peoria, and it used a five-mile railroad to reach from the pit to the prep plant alongside the Minneapolis & St. Louis Railroad. It bought a small fleet of surplus M&StL 0-6-0 switch engines to shuttle the coal trains back and forth between the loader and the prep plant. Special hopper cars were used with automatic bottom dumps actuated by a truck tire that would ride up on a ramp rail at the dumper. Two locomotives would shuttle three sets of cars between the loader, where large trucks would deliver the raw coal from the pit, and the dumper at the tipple, where the coal was cleaned, graded, and loaded into outbound M&StL hoppers.

This was one of the last regular steam operations in Illinois, lasting into the early 1960s. When steam was retired, the railroad was shut down, and the trucks then delivered the coal directly from the pit to the tipple. The railroad was based upon the technology and economics of the 1940s, but even with steam power and that short haul, the railroad was more economical to operate than the larger fleet of trucks and drivers that would have been required to replace it. When the cost of operating the old locomotives became prohibitive, however, it was cheaper to expand the truck fleet than replace the steam engines with diesels.

One of the largest mining operations in Illinois is the Peabody Coal Company's River King complex near St. Louis. The Randolph Preparation Plant, looming like a lost skyscraper in the cornfields, is fed by conveyors from the Baldwin No. 1 underground mine and the River King No. 6 surface mine—the River King's electric shovels are among the largest ever built. The Randolph Prep Plant provides cleaned coal for the Baldwin Power Plant, only three miles away, as well as the Kaskaskia River barge terminal of the Kaskaskia River Port District (KRPD), about ten miles away.

In the mid-1970s, the River King operation was particularly interesting since the Baldwin Power Plant trains were pale yellow Peabody hoppers pulled by veteran Baldwin diesels, while the KRPD trains were bright red hoppers powered by ex-Frisco GP7s. The KRPD cars had five air-operated hopper bays under each car, while the Peabody cars had longitudinal hopper doors running the length of the cars. The power plant not only took two 12-car shuttles from the Randolph Prep Plant for 16 hours every day, but it would also bring in one entire unit train per day off the Gulf, Mobile & Ohio out of Southwestern Illinois Coal's Streamline Mine at Percy, Illinois!

COAL AND ELECTRICITY

Power plants burn coal to generate electricity, and sometimes that electricity is used to move the coal. Up to this time, nearly all North American railroad electrification had been accomplished with power generated by the railroad itself, usually at a unique frequency or voltage that was suited to the type of service or locomotives employed. In the 1960s, the power generating industry was exploring the potential of getting the railroads to purchase its power right off the commercial "grids," and new technology was being developed to make high voltage (25,000 volts) "commercial frequency" (60 cycles) alternating current, which was being adopted in Europe but generally ignored in this country.

The American Electric Coal Company was at that time building a new power plant in southwestern Ohio near its Muskingum coal mine. AEP got together with General Electric to use the 15-mile railroad between the mine and power plant as a test bed for future mainline electrification. GE produced two 5,000-hp road-switchers that could convert the 25,000-volt AC current into standard 600-volt DC traction motors and strung the line with the latest design of economical overhead trolley wire.

The Muskingum Electric Railroad opened in 1968 with its bright red-and-white locomotives

The Midland Electric Coal Corporation had a tipple and prep plant at Middle Grove, Illinois, that was supplied with raw coal from a strip mine five miles away. They used a railroad and a small fleet of ex-Minneapolis & St. Louis 0-6-0 switch engines to shuttle the coal cars back and forth. Here on a typical day in 1959, engine 81 is easing down the hill with the train of loads, while the 85 is beginning its noisy run to the top of the hill in the distance with the empties. Once over that hump, it was nearly flat and straight for the rest of the run to the loader near the pit. On the high tracks in the background are M&StL hoppers that will carry the outbound coal from the prep plant.

shuttling 12-car coal trains between the loader loop at the mine and the dumping bridge at the power plant. Soon the entire operation was automated, and the trains made their over-the-road runs with no crew members aboard the train, with speeds reaching 55 MPH. The Muskingum was a great success, and by the twenty-first century nearly every mainline electrification in the country had converted to its commercial frequency AC power.

In the Arizona desert, the 78-mile Black Mesa & Lake Powell was opened in 1973 to carry coal from the Black Mesa Mine to the Navajo Generating Station using a 50,000-volt commercial frequency system that permitted the entire line to be supplied by a single substation. Three 6,000-hp GE E60 locomotives could run 72 MPH over the road with a 10,000-ton coal train.

ANTHRACITE TODAY

In the late 1800s the Philadelphia & Reading had created an industrial empire out of the mining and transportation of anthracite coal. Even in the twenty-first century, scissors-bed dump trucks can be found around Scranton delivering the clean-burning anthracite to the coal bins of residential homes, and in the winter the region is fragrant with the pleasant aroma of coal furnaces.

But for the most part, fuel oil and natural gas have replaced anthracite for home heating. By the early 1950s, the bottom had literally dropped out of the economy of the "anthracite region" of Pennsylvania, and the once numerous anthracite "breakers" (the anthracite term for a prep plant) began to come down. There was nowhere enough business to support the massive infrastructure of the coal region lines, and anthracite-dependent railroads like the Reading, Lehigh Valley, and Delaware, Lackawanna & Western were soon all merged into Conrail.

In 1990, Andy Muller, a shortline entrepreneur and unabashed fan of steam locomotives, drastically expanded his ten-mile tourist-hauling Blue Mountain & Reading by acquiring from Conrail 134 miles of former Reading anthracite lines in the heart of the coal region between Reading and Scranton. He purchased a fleet of used diesel

The only place you will find electric locomotives pulling freight today is on captive industrial operations like the 78-mile Black Mesa & Lake Powell in Arizona, which carries coal from the Black Mesa Mine to the Navajo Generating Station. A loaded 10,000-ton coal train is eastbound near Kayenta, Arizona, in June 1987. ALEX MAYES

On April 6, 1991, Shortline president Andy Muller put his ex-Reading T1 4-8-4 No. 2102 on a Reading & Northern coal train out of Tamaqua, Pennsylvania, carrying 35 100-ton cars of high grade anthracite (the equivalent of a 70-car train of steam-era hoppers) bound for interchange with Conrail at Reading. The coal would be taken to the pier at Philadelphia for shipment by ocean vessel to Quebec Iron & Titanium to be made into paint pigment. But the statistics were incidental as Andy opened the throttle, and the 2102 accelerated noisily through New Ringgold. For a moment, 1940s freight railroading had returned to the little Pennsylvania burgh.

locomotives and painted them into a livery similar to that of the former Reading Company, as he put them to work hauling anthracite out of the traditional Reading breakers and delivering it to Conrail on the north side of the city of Reading.

To celebrate the opening of his new Blue Mountain, Reading & Northern on the April 5–6 weekend in 1991, he fired up his tourist-hauling former Reading Class T1 4-8-4 No. 2102 and put it to work on a real coal-gathering job. On the dreary Saturday, the 2102 wonderfully recreated the atmosphere of working steam days. The 4-8-4 had been built in 1945 in the company's big locomotive shop in Reading and had spent much of its working life on the lines radiating out of there.

Since there was no way to turn the 4-8-4 at either end of the run, it began work on Saturday by picking up a train of empty hoppers off Conrail at Belt Line Junction and backing tender-first up to Port Clinton with nine Conrail 100-ton hoppers and three loaded covered hoppers. As it began to get dark in the evening, the 2102 spotted a covered hopper of malt at the Yuengling Beer brewery at Pottsville before "tying up" for the night at the old coal junction yard of West Cressona.

On the sunny Sunday morning, the 2102 returned to Port Clinton and then backed up

another former-Reading line to Tamaqua, where 35 100-ton loads of anthracite out of the Lehigh Coal & Navigation Company's Greenwood Breaker were waiting to be taken to the Conrail seaport at Philadelphia. This was part of a 220-car shipment that was bound for "Vessel No.1," the first of ten shipments for 1991 bound for the Quebec Iron & Titanium mill on the St. Lawrence River where it would be used to make white paint pigment (please don't ask how you get white paint out of black coal—there are some things in chemistry that are better left a mystery).

The black 4-8-4 put on a wonderful show moving the coal south from Tamaqua. Five more loads for Vessel No. 1 were added at Port Clinton to bring the consist up to 40 cars, capped off with a traditional red caboose. Since there were modern 100-ton hoppers, the 4,000-ton train was the equivalent of an 80-car train of 50-ton steam-era hoppers. As the 2102 and its coal train romped through Leesport at 40 MPH with its whistle screaming, the Golden Age of "King Coal" was recreated for a brief moment on a balmy April afternoon. But that 4,000 tons of anthracite was on revenue waybills and bound for a very real customer. Not all that much had changed in 150 years.

The Republic Steel works in Cleveland, Ohio, is served by the River Terminal Railway. In October 1968, the shiny exteriors of brand new Electro-Motive SW1001s 101 and 102 are in stark contrast to the rusty environment of the huge mill complex. These locomotives are used to move everything from hot billets to rolled sheet among the various processing buildings, as well as bringing in raw materials and moving out finished product.

6

Iron and
Steel

*I*ron is a lot like coal, only heavier. Railroads and steel mills created the "smokestack America" of the early twentieth century and were the very foundation of the Industrial Revolution. Coal is an essential element in the steel industry, and railroads handle iron ore in much the same manner as they do coal. In colonial America, iron ore was found in such unlikely places as Massachusetts, New Jersey, and Pennsylvania, and smelting furnaces were

Along the Cuyahoga River in downtown Cleveland in October 1968, the River Terminal Railway shoves a string of empty hoppers into the loading tracks beneath the Hulett unloaders where iron ore is removed from the cargo holds of the lake boats. These cars will then be moved to various places within the Republic Steel works or interchanged to a mainline railroad for shipment to other mills. At facilities like this, the hoppers often bring in coal and carry out iron ore brought down from Minnesota.

usually small, local affairs located near the sources of the ore. There was little real understanding of the chemical processes involved, and the native ores varied widely in quality and properties. During the Revolutionary War, for instance, the smelter at Andover, New Jersey, was of great strategic value because the nearby ore yielded the only iron in the colonies that could be drawn into wire. Not surprisingly, a few decades later, one of the first railroads in the state was a narrow-gauge tramway that used mules to haul the carloads of Andover iron to the Morris Canal, a few miles away at Waterloo.

Pig iron is created by heating the ore in a charcoal-fueled fire along with limestone, to draw out some of the impurities. The charcoal provided a source of carbon to improve the chemical content and working capabilities of the iron. Steel is created when the hard and brittle pig iron is melted at high temperatures with a source of even more carbon, like charcoal, which is made from wood. Until the mid-1800s, this was a laborious and expensive process, and steel was reserved for only the most necessary tools and weapons. Cast and wrought iron was used for such workaday items as structural material, rails and castings.

Following the Civil War, however, the technology of steel-making took some giant strides with the development of the Bessemer converter and the open-hearth furnace. Coke made from coal replaced charcoal, and huge industrial steel mills began to spring up along the waterways of the Northeast and Great Lakes. In Minnesota, Michigan, and Wisconsin, huge deposits of high-grade iron ore stretching for hundreds of miles were discovered on both sides of Lake Superior, and the pattern was set for industrial America.

In the late 1880s, railroads reached into the iron ranges from ports on Lake Superior and Lake Michigan, and huge steam-powered boats were designed to carry the heavy iron ore to steel mills and railheads on the lower lakes. (Incidentally, the bulk carriers on the Great Lakes are referred to as "boats;" the term "ship" is reserved for ocean-going vessels.) The navigation locks at Sault Ste. Marie and elsewhere tamed the confluences of the lakes and made water transport both practical and cost-effective. Since the railroads and lake boats developed closely as a unified transportation system, to this day they exhibit a degree of intermodal standardization that is remarkable in the transportation field. The ore docks where railcars

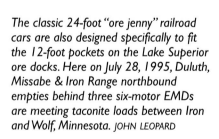

The classic 24-foot "ore jenny" railroad cars are also designed specifically to fit the 12-foot pockets on the Lake Superior ore docks. Here on July 28, 1995, Duluth, Missabe & Iron Range northbound empties behind three six-motor EMDs are meeting taconite loads between Iron and Wolf, Minnesota. JOHN LEOPARD

are unloaded into the lake boats were standardized with "pockets" on 12-foot centers with loading chutes for the boats. The boat cargo hold hatches, on 24-foot centers, were designed to match the chutes, and the railroad "ore jenny" hoppers were standardized at 24 feet in length to line up with the 12-foot pockets. A long cut of coupled ore jennies would align their hopper dumps over every other twelve-foot pocket. As the ore jennies grew in size over the years from 20 up to 70 tons, they simply got "taller" and stronger but retained the same 24-foot length!

Probably the most famous of the ore-hauling railroads is the Duluth, Missabe & Iron Range, which reaches north from Duluth and Two Harbors, Minnesota, into the Vermilion and Missabe iron ranges. In the days of steam, the DM&IR was famous for its fleet of huge and handsome 2-8-8-4 "Yellowstone" articulateds, which were built by

Baldwin in the early 1940s and could handle trains of 190 70-ton loaded ore jennies.

Most of the ore was dug from huge strip mines, many of which had sloping terraces and miles of railroad spiraling downward to the working faces. While the DM&IR was the biggest ore-hauler, other railroads like the Great Northern, the Soo Line, the Chicago & North Western, and the Lake Superior & Ishpeming tapped the iron ranges in Minnesota and upper Michigan.

In the same fashion that coal customers would blend different grades of coal into the holds of ships at tidewater, steel mills would specify specific blends of iron ore for the lake boats. On the DM&IR, "mixing bowl" yards at Proctor and Two Harbors would line up trains for the ore docks that would contain the proper mix to be loaded into a specific vessel's hold. Each pocket on an ore dock will hold four carloads, 280 tons, and a "standard"

Iron ore dug out of the Missabe Range begins its water journey to steel mills in the lower states at "pocket docks" like this one on Lake Superior in Duluth. Here on July 16, 1991, the Duluth, Missabe & Iron Range's "1530 Dock Switch" job is spotting ore cars above the Canada Steamship Lines bulk carrier Lemoyne, *which is a standard 730-foot lake boat designed specifically to fit this type of loading dock. JOHN LEOPARD*

late steam-era 730-foot boat would hold about 360 carloads for a cargo of 25,000 tons. Most of the traditional pocket docks were built to 1,500 or more feet in length over the water to be able to accommodate two 730-foot boats on each side.

Over the years the lake boats grew larger, while maintaining the 12-foot dock chute standard. The monsters of today are 1,000-foot vessels carrying 60,000 tons or 860 carloads of ore. It takes about twelve hours to load a 1,000-foot boat from a pocket dock. Some of the newer ore loading facilities have replaced the long pocket docks with conveyor systems that can load a 1,000-footer in about four hours. A fully loaded ore boat will draw 27 feet of water at the keel. And just in case you think your sport utility vehicle is a gas-guzzler, a 1,000-foot ore boat, powered by four General Motors/EMD 20-cylinder 645 diesel engines (the same prime mover as the EMD 3,600-hp SD45) gets 45 gallons to the mile! Because of their convenient standard size, however, and ability to get into some of the smaller harbors, there are still a few of the 730-foot boats on the lakes.

UNLOADING THE BOATS

It is easy to see how ore from jennies can be dumped into pocket docks and then poured into the hold of a boat, but how do you get all that red stuff back on dry land when gravity is now working against you? In the old days they did it the hard way: by hand. An army of laborers with shovels would scoop the ore into buckets, which would be hoisted out of the hold.

Then in 1910 "the monsters" arrived on the scene and drastically speeded up the process. The "Hulett Unloader" was a giant crane with counterbalanced "walking beams" that carried a clamshell bucket at the end of a vertical shaft. The operator rode the shaft up and down in a control cabin right above the bucket for optimum visibility. Each scoop would lift 17 tons of ore out of the hold and place it on a shuttle car or conveyor belt, where it could be weighed and then dispatched to a railroad car or stockpile. The first Huletts were steam-powered, but soon electric motors took over. A boat that required 33 hours to unload by bucket could be cleaned out by a Hulett in five hours.

Many steel mills were built right on the lakefront in places like Gary, Indiana, and Lorain and Cleveland, Ohio, where the lake boats could pull right into the facility to unload. For ore bound for mills elsewhere, like Pittsburgh, or Youngstown, Ohio, or Bethlehem, Pennsylvania, the ore was loaded into railroad cars from ports like Conneaut or Ashtabula, Ohio, all of which had rows of Huletts. For ore bound from ship to rail, however, there were no pocket docks or need for 24-foot cars, and most inland-bound ore moved in conventional coal hoppers. Since iron ore is much heavier and more concentrated than coal, however, a 70-ton hopper would appear to be only partially loaded, with just a dollop of ore atop each hopper bay—the total weight, however, would equal that of a full visible

Following the Civil War, the huge iron ranges in Minnesota, Michigan, and Wisconsin replaced New Jersey and Pennsylvania as the primary source for iron ore in the U.S. The Missabe Range was so huge, and the ore was so close to the surface, that strip mining made operations very economical, compared to the deep mines in the Northeast. In the 1940s, steam locomotives were being used by the Oliver Iron Mining Company in terraced open-pit mines like this one. The side-dump cars would deliver ore to a preparation plant, where it would be cleaned and graded for loading into DM&IR ore jennies for movement south to the huge docks on Lake Superior.
RAILFAN & RAILROAD *COLLECTION*

One of the busiest ore ports on Lake Erie is the Pittsburgh & Conneaut Dock Company facility at Conneaut, Ohio, served by the Bessemer & Lake Erie, which has a main line direct to Pittsburgh. In October 1968, a B&LE Baldwin diesel was working the loading tracks beneath the massive Hulett unloaders.

load of coal. While full trains of 24-foot ore jennies would sometimes be found in the lower states away from the lakes, it was much more common to see it moving in conventional coal cars.

In the mid-twentieth century, United States Steel had a vast industrial empire of mines, mills, and railways. It owned the DM&IR from the ore pits to the lake, and it also owned the Bessemer & Lake Erie, which is a thoroughfare for ore from Conneaut, Ohio, to the hungry mills of Pittsburgh. And the Bessemer had the best of both worlds, because it hauled Appalachian coal north to the lake for shipment to power plants and steel mills and loaded the same hoppers back south with iron ore for Pittsburgh.

One major factor in the handling of Great Lakes ore traffic is the weather. The harbors and narrows of the upper Great Lakes are frozen over more than four months out of the year, and even the most powerful boats are unable to navigate. Rather than revert to all-rail routes in the winter, however, the entire industry is geared toward delivering twelve months of product in less than eight months and stockpiling the ore and coal at their destinations. Once they are fired up, blast furnaces will often run seven or eight years, 24 hours a day, being constantly tapped and recharged. Thus, stockpiles of coal, iron and limestone become essential for wintertime operation.

TACONITE TODAY

World War II put a tremendous strain on the Minnesota ore region, and by the end of hostilities, much of the rich, easy-to-mine ore had been used up, having been the source for 85 percent of America's iron. There were many grades of ore, however, and billions of tons of the lower-grade taconite remained in the ground, often in the same pits, where it had been pushed aside to get at the higher-quality ores. In the 1950s, a washing, magnetic separation, and sintering process was developed to economically extract the 15–30 percent ore from the raw taconite. In this process, the ore was blended with bentonite clay into marble-sized pellets for shipment. By 1980, taconite pellets accounted for more than 90 percent of American ore shipments. (Taconite ore pellets are considerably easier to load and unload, and freezing is less of a problem in winter.)

Meanwhile, new iron ranges north of the St. Lawrence River in Canada were being tapped, and new isolated railroads were built along the north shore of Lake Superior to reach taconite fields. Many of the new facilities used conveyor-style ship loading rather than pocket docks.

A new breed of postwar ore boats soon rendered the Hulett unloaders obsolete, as they were "self-unloaders" with conveyors at the bottoms of their cargo holds and conveyor booms topside. By

Because they do not need to be used on the standard pocket docks, conventional coal hoppers are often used to handle iron ore south of the lakes. Here in October 1968, a trainload of ore, probably from the seaport at Philadelphia and bound for Johnstown or Pittsburgh, is laboring up the famous Horseshoe Curve west of Altoona, Pennsylvania. Because the iron ore is much more dense than coal, the ore is loaded in two humps atop the trucks. Although they appear to be partial loads, these cars are carrying their maximum weight. The locomotives are mid-train helpers, and two more units are pushing on the rear end.

the end of the twentieth century, there wasn't a Hulett left in service on the lakes.

Since the self-unloaders are generally larger, more efficient, and faster to unload, the overall fleet of bulk carriers has dwindled from over 250 to less than 60. Of course, the big boats carry far more than just iron ore, as many are dedicated to cement and grain service, and the ore carriers can get return loads of coal from the same lower lake ports where they deliver the iron. The opening of the St. Lawrence Seaway in 1958 extended the potential range of bulk-carrier service nearly to the Atlantic Ocean. But wherever they went, the big lake boats always dealt with a railroad interface at one end of the run or the other—and often at both ends.

RAILROADS IN THE MILLS

It takes two tons of iron ore, a half a ton of coke, and another half ton of limestone and miscellaneous additives like scrap metal to produce one ton of pig iron in a blast furnace. Sooner or later, all of that raw material moves by rail.

Within the rust-colored boundaries of the mills themselves, rails usually play an important role in moving the raw material in, the molten pig iron from the blast furnaces to the steel converters, the ingots to the finishing mills, and the end products out to market. Typically, hordes of switch engines shove hot bottle cars of molten iron from building to building and open pots of lava-like slag out to the cooling pits—slag dumping at night is one of the most impressive sights in all of railroading. In the 1970s, the use of new continuous casting machines reduced much of the hot ingot rail transfer within the mills.

Even in today's environmentally conscious facilities, steel-making is a grimy and dirty business. Railroad equipment that "lives" within the confines of the mills usually takes on the rusty patina of everything in the plant.

The world still has an insatiable appetite for steel, but new technology has changed the character of "smokestack America." New processes like the Basic Oxygen Furnace and continuous casting, combined with computerized monitoring and quality control, have made steel mills much less labor intensive. Many of the new technologies, however, could not be applied to existing older facilities, and new high-tech mills in both the U.S. and around the world began replacing the industrial giants of the past. Today the Mahoning Valley of Youngstown is completely barren of the towering blast furnaces, and Pittsburgh is no longer

RIGHT: Modern processing methods can extract high-grade iron ore from taconite, which was previously pushed aside as worthless. Here on January 29, 1991, a DM&IR train is loading at the Fairland, Minnesota, pellet plant of Eveleth Taconite Company. JOHN LEOPARD

BELOW: The Erie Mining Company built new facilities to process and load taconite. This huge bridge at Taconite Harbor, on June 11, 1991, is part of a balloon loop that parallels the shore of Lake Superior, where the boats are loaded by conveyors. JOHN LEOPARD

The Republic Steel works in Cleveland, Ohio, uses River Terminal Railway locomotives to move both raw hot steel and finished products around the various buildings in the sprawling complex, shown here in October 1968.

RIGHT: As steel-making technology changed over the years, some steel mills had no room to grow "on site" and had to put new processes some distance away. The Armco Steel mill at New Miami, Ohio, would move molten iron from its old blast furnaces to the new Basic Oxygen Furnace steel plant in trains of "bottle cars" like this one, photographed on November 22, 1984. The steel shells of the cars are protected from the molten iron by a thick lining of firebrick. They are emptied by rotating to pour. BRADLEY McCLELLAND

covered with smoky clag. But the modern environmentally friendly mills along the Great Lakes and elsewhere keep cranking out thousands of tons of sheet, slab, rod, and coil steel that are moved over the railroads to manufacturers and construction sites everywhere.

Some steel mills turn out finished products, such as structural beams, rails, wire, nails, reinforcing rods, pipe, and tubing, while others produce raw steel in standardized forms like sheets, slabs, bars, and coils that can be shipped to manufacturers or fabricating plants. Automobile plants, for instance, make extensive use of machines that take standard-sized coils of thin sheet steel in one end and spit everything from auto frames to fenders out the other. Consider some of the everyday items that are made from steel: electric power transmission towers, oil tanks, entire refineries, automobiles, office furniture, household appliances, airplanes, farm machinery, sheet roofing and siding, springs, fencing, nuts and bolts, guitar strings and paper clips, furnaces and air conditioners, bicycles and motorcycles, ships and boats, roller bearings and army tanks, and locomotives and freight cars themselves. Even the machines and tools that make the microchips for your computer.

This outbound steel is most often transported in open gondola or flatcars. Some customers want coil steel that has not been exposed to the weath-

er, however, and that is shipped in special flatcars with vee-shaped bottom racks and removable lids to protect the load. Although many are shipped in convenient lengths for gondolas or flatcars, many huge structural beams for bridge and building construction can move out as loads straddling as many as three flatcars. Tubes and pipe usually go out in long gondola cars, while smaller products like wire and nails are packaged for easy handling and shipped in boxcars.

Like the railroads themselves, the steel mills that shaped America have changed and become less visible to the casual observer, but that timeless team of trains and steel continues to drive the industrial economy of the world.

Many modern factories, like automobile plants, have fabricating machinery that is designed to use standard-sized coils of steel. In the 1960s, the railroads came up with special flatcars created specifically for carrying steel coils in a trough-like floor. The protective lids are completely removed for loading and unloading. These brand-new cars were built in 1966 for the Illinois Central Railroad.

In the latter decades of the twentieth century, many American steel mills shut down as steel technology changed dramatically, and the old plants did not lend themselves to modernization. Instead of smelting raw ore, it became more economical to recycle, and scrap steel became a very big business. Here in 1999, the New York Cross Harbor Railroad floats a barge loaded with gondolas full of scrap steel across New York Harbor from Brooklyn to the old Pennsylvania Railroad float yard at Greenville, New Jersey. JOE GREENSTEIN

The boxcars were comin' and goin' in August 1969, as eastbound freights on the Chicago, Burlington & Quincy and Rock Island crossed over and under at Wyanet, Illinois. These were the last "glory days" of the boxcar, before the modern steel 50-footers began to give up their loads to "piggyback" highway truck trailers on flatcars. This scene in the middle of the cornfields demonstrates the best in American railroading, as boxcars from the UP and N&W are speeding toward Chicago on competing railroads.

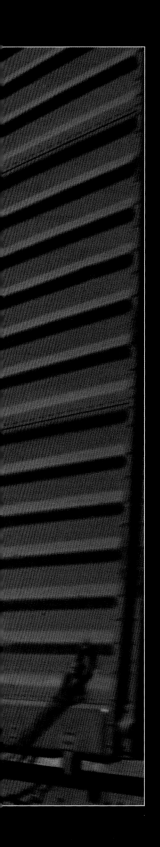

7

Boxcar Business

Boxcar business did not begin with a boxcar. The idea of hauling "general freight" dates back centuries before the railroads. The necessities of life like food and building materials were traditionally moved overland by pack animals or in wagons. The goods were put into containers that could be handled by one or two men, and by the 1700s wooden barrels were among the most popular because even heavily loaded they could be rolled along the ground

By the spring of 1985, the "boxcar" had morphed into the piggyback trailer riding on a flatcar. A decade earlier, the contents of that Southern Pacific "Golden Pig Service" trailer would likely have been riding in a boxcar. The piggyback car did not replace the flatcar, it replaced the boxcar. In the 1980s the railroads were still exploring the optimum type of flatcar to use for such "intermodal" service, and one option was this lightweight single-trailer flat that brought the four-wheel railroad car back onto America's main lines. The Golden Pig Service was named for the SP's famous Chicago–Los Angeles "Golden State Route" for passenger trains.

A classic outside-braced wooden boxcar of the World War I era has been preserved at the Steamtown National Historic Site in Scranton, Pennsylvania. Here on November 3, 1990, the Central Vermont boxcar clearly shows its wooden construction. Note how the door hangs from the top rail and has only hook-like guides on the bottom. The car rides on early Andrews trucks that are now outlawed for interchange service. The steam locomotive is Steamtown's 0-6-0 No. 26, which had spent most of its working life as one of the switch engines in the Eddystone locomotive factory of the Baldwin Locomotive Works.

by a single laborer. They could carry almost anything, wet or dry, and be loaded into wagons or canal boats or sailing ships—or railroad cars.

The earliest freight cars in both England and the U.S. were simple four-wheeled flatcars, often with low sides to keep the barrels from sliding off (these were later called "gondola" cars). The Baltimore & Ohio had a fleet of these "flour cars" that could carry 24 barrels of flour from mills in the rural Maryland countryside to the thriving port city of Baltimore. Almost anything else could be packed into barrels or boxes and loaded on the cars. If protection from the weather was desired, a canvas tarpaulin was tied over the top of the load.

Since railroads were "invented" in England in an already highly populated urban setting, the locomotives burned coal or coke from the very beginning. In the heavily forested colonies, however, wood was the cheapest and most abundant fuel. The only problem with wood fuel for a locomotive is that instead of relatively benign cinders, the exhaust produces an incredible shower of hot embers that land on everything and tend to set hundreds of tiny fires, some of which become very big fires. The embers could also ignite the wooden barrels or bales of cotton and even more readily set fire to a dry tarp, with all its inviting folds.

In 1833, the Mohawk & Hudson Railroad created a covered gondola with a permanent wooden roof, and the boxcar was born. The M&H paralleled the Erie Canal and did its most vigorous business in the dead of winter, when the canal was frozen over. It is not surprising that they would want a better way to protect the load from the weather. These early four-wheelers looked like small houses, and the idea of such "house cars" quickly became popular in America.

The rigid four-wheel undercarriage, popular in England, was soon abandoned in America, where the distances were much greater and the trackwork less sophisticated. A car with two four-wheel trucks would be much more flexible and provide a much better ride on the wilderness railroads. The standardizing of coupler heights for interchange resulted in a uniformity of floor heights and general dimensions for boxcars, flats, and gondolas by the 1850s, and freighthouses and loading platforms soon sprang up all along the railroads.

The typical Civil War-era boxcar could carry about 20 tons of payload and was about 28 feet long. Construction was of wood with a heavy beamed framework and a large sliding center

door on each side. Iron "truss rods" strengthened the underframes, and turnbuckles in the center could be tightened to keep the car from sagging as the wood aged and compressed from continuous service.

The boxcar was easy to load from a lineside platform or a wagon, and it could carry virtually anything and protect it from the weather. Everything had to be loaded by hand, so the lading was usually in 50-to-200-pound boxes or barrels. With the door in the center of the sides, the loads would be shoved to the ends of the cars where the weight would be naturally concentrated above the trucks. Since the car's interior was wood, the load could be secured with bracing that was simply nailed into the floor and walls. Boxcars could carry bales of cotton, coal in bags, and oil in barrels, as well as all forms of dry goods in all sorts of packaging. Long lumber was generally loaded by hand, being angled through the doors and simply stacked on the floor until the car was filled. By nailing temporary wooden "grain doors" across the doorways, boxcars could even be loaded with bulk grain. They were truly the universal railroad car.

As the railroads grew in the late 1800s, so did the boxcar. Because it was a "cubic" container, the boxcar became more efficient as it got bigger. The volume and load capacity of a car increased much

more rapidly as it got bigger than did the cost and weight of the carbody construction. Cars that were intended to carry relatively lightweight but space-consuming goods like furniture and even new wagons became quite large. The size of the doors would often determine or limit what could be loaded, and some cars were also fitted with full-size end doors for easier loading of things like buggies.

The boxcar even influenced the growth and physical appearance and layout of towns and cities. Local businesses would build their factories and mills along the railroad so that they could have access to private sidings for loading and unloading cars. Businesses not sited directly on the tracks could use the railroad's freighthouse or "team track." A team track was simply a siding with an adjacent flat road and parking area where wagons could be brought alongside for transfer of cargo.

One of the oldest iron boxcars in existence is this Baltimore & Ohio curved-side 17000 in the B&O Museum in Baltimore. Although the exact history of this car cannot be documented, it is a genuine article, probably built in the 1880s, based on the Thatcher Perkins design from the 1860s. It rides today on trucks of a slightly more recent vintage. Iron cars like this were used during the Civil War to transport gunpowder.

The availability of rail transportation had a profound effect upon the growing nation. Without transportation, nearly everything had to be produced locally, from furniture to cooking pots to clothing. With the availability of economical transportation, factories could be set up to efficiently manufacture items in large quantities which could then be distributed to customers nationwide. Everyday items could be manufactured in the cities and distributed to stores throughout the mountains and prairies, and raw material could be brought in to a factory from a wide variety of sources. The entire complexion of commerce was changing in the late 1800s. And nearly all of it sooner or later rode in a boxcar.

STEEL BOXCARS

Boxcars were always a compromise between cost and durability, and because they often traveled far from home, some degree of standardized construction and the availability of repair parts was desirable. As early as the 1850s some railroads were experimenting with iron boxcars that could be used for transporting gunpowder. While the iron cars were essentially fireproof, they tended to "sweat" with changes in humidity and temperature and were not widely embraced by the railroads.

The development of the steel industry in the late 1800s, however, brought the metal freight cars back into vogue. The availability of inexpensive sheet steel and the advent of air-powered metal-working tools encouraged many railroads to experiment with steel cars. By 1890, the general condition of the trackwork had improved enough to handle the larger locomotives, and therefore heavier cars could also be considered. Here again, the cubic aspect of the boxcar worked in favor of larger cars, as payload increased with size much faster than construction and material weight and costs. You could transport that same load in 50 30-ton wooden cars as you could in 30 newer and larger 50-ton steel cars—but the steel train would be overall less weight and shorter in length.

The term "steel car" can be a bit misleading, however, for it was not until after World War II that wood was completely eliminated from freight cars, particularly boxcars. A car could have a steel underframe, side trusses, and sheeting, as well as roofs and ends, and still have wood lining for the floors and inside walls.

Although the industry could not agree on a standard boxcar design, by the 1920s most had grown to 40 feet in length with a capacity of about 50 tons. The most popular cars of this era were the standard 40-foot boxcar adopted by the USRA (the United States Railway Administration, which took over the railroads during World War I) and the famous Pennsylvania Railroad "X29."

In 1932 the Association of American Railroads designed a new all-steel 40-foot boxcar that was a bit taller than the USRA and X29, and with a 50-ton capacity, it quickly became the industry favorite. In 1947, the Pullman-Standard Company refined the AAR boxcar with some aircraft design techniques for strengthening the underframe, sides, ends, and roof while lightening the overall construction. The "PS-1" became the industry's first truly standard boxcar, and Pullman permitted other manufacturers to build cars to its design.

Those Boxcar Slogans

By middle of the twentieth century, just about every railroad had a slogan. They were used in advertising and on timetables and the like, and were often emblazoned on the sides of boxcars as well. Reading all these slogans as a long freight clanked past was part of the fun of train-watching.

Quite often the slogans extolled each road's highly competitive passenger service. Union Pacific's "Road of the Streamliners" is a good example, and appropriate, too, for UP fielded the first true lightweight streamliner. Chicago, Burlington & Quincy—another streamliner pioneer—touted its fleet of shiny silver *Zephyrs* serving the West and Midwest on countless boxcars: "Way of the *Zephyrs*." The Burlington also used another slogan that referred to the geographic area it served: "Everywhere West." Other roads also used geographic slogans to good advantage. New York Central's "Water Level Route" phrase referred to its easy-grade New York–Chicago main line that followed river valleys around the mountains rather than climbing over them as did rival Pennsylvania Railroad. Central also employed slogans to promote its famous fast freights, the most familiar being the "Pacemaker Freight Service" that adorned its snappy fleet of red-and-gray boxcars in the 1940s and 1950s.

Like New York Central, many other railroads used multiple slogans to promote their various lines and services. The Chicago & North Western even used a different slogan on each side of the same car! Back in an era when there were dozens of colorful railroads competing for traffic, the following slogans were commonly seen on long passing freights.

The Chicago, Burlington & Quincy made dramatic use of the billboard potential of its freight cars with a wide variety of slogans like "Way of the Zephyrs" and "Everywhere West," shown here at Rochelle, Illinois. On this day in 1965 the CB&Q put 2-8-2 4960 on its regular mixed train from Aurora to Oregon, Illinois.

Fast Freight Route (Western Maryland)
High Speed Service (Nickel Plate Road)
Speedway to America's Playground (Florida East Coast)
Route of the "400" Streamliners (Chicago & North Western)
The Road Of Anthracite (Delaware, Lackawanna & Western)
Route of the Black Diamond (Lehigh Valley)
Feather River Route (Western Pacific)
The Right Way (Central of Georgia)
The Only Way (Alton Railroad)
Pine Tree Route (Maine Central)
Route of the Empire Builder (Great Northern)
Golden State Route (Rock Island and Southern Pacific)
Linking 13 Great States With The Nation (Baltimore & Ohio)
Friendly Service Route (Erie Lackawanna)
Route Of Courteous Service (Seaboard Air Line Railroad)
Road of Personalized Services (Illinois Terminal)
Main Line of Mid-America (Illinois Central)
Mainline Thru The Rockies (Denver & Rio Grande Western)
Main Street Of The Northwest (Northern Pacific)
The Northwest's Own Railway (Spokane Portland & Seattle)

The Bridge Line (Delaware & Hudson)
The Chicago Line (Chicago & Eastern Illinois)
Connects With All Chicago Railroads (Indiana Harbor Belt)
Serves The South (Southern Railway)
Sooner Through The Southwest (Kansas, Oklahoma & Gulf)
Quicker Via Peoria (Peoria & Eastern)
The Peoria Road (Toledo Peoria & Western)
The Peoria Gateway (Minneapolis & St. Louis)
The St. Louis Gateway (Litchfield & Madison)
Green Mountain Gateway (Rutland Railroad)
Ship And Travel Santa Fe All The Way (Santa Fe)
The Sole Leather Line (Wellsville, Addison & Galeton)
The Hoosier Line (Monon)
The Dixie Line (Louisville & Nashville)
The Rebel Route (Gulf, Mobile & Ohio)
Blue Streak Fast Freight Service (Cotton Belt Route)
Follow The Flag (Wabash)
Corn Belt Route (Chicago Great Western)
Route of the Eagles (Missouri Pacific)
Route of the Rockets (Chicago, Rock Island & Pacific)
Serves the Steel Centers (Pittsburg & Lake Erie)
Route of the Minuteman (Boston & Maine)
Route of the Dashing Commuter (Long Island Rail Road)
The Good Track Road (Grand Trunk Western)
Serves All the West (Union Pacific)

There were many more slogans in use over the years. Some were used over a long period of time, and others were not. Along with the railroad name they told you something more about the railroad itself—where it was, what it did, and what it was best known for.

The Bangor & Aroostook Railroad was famous for its colorful boxcars. The red, white and blue "State of Maine Products" livery, shown in the distance, dates from the 1950s, while the cars in the foreground are modern variations. These cars were being spotted at the Great Northern Paper mill in East Millinocket, Maine, in 1978.

This is not to say that by the 1940s all boxcars were alike. Quite the contrary. Nearly every railroad home shop had its own idea of what a boxcar should look like, and the variations were infinite. Carbuilders competed with each other to sell components like ends and doors, which the home shops applied with wild mix-and-match abandon. The Santa Fe liked heavy fishbelly truss underframes, while you could spot a distinctive B&O "wagon top" car from a mile away. During World War II, restrictions on steel supplies found many railroads and carbuilders returning to "composite" cars with steel frames and wood sides, which resulted in wooden cars still roaming the rails into the 1970s.

The big slab sides of the boxcars provided the railroads with an unexpected pubic-relations tool: they made superb rolling billboards. From the earliest fleets, the railroads would put their names in huge and colorful letters and heralds or logos on the car sides. Some enterprising railroads even tried to sell boxcar sides as advertising space, but this practice was banned to prevent one shipper from having to load his goods into a car advertising his competitor. The railroads themselves, however, could use the cars to pitch their own passenger trains or freight service.

Since cost was always a factor, boxcars were traditionally painted in a durable and economical oxide red, a brownish color that became known as "boxcar red." The more colorful pigments were more expensive to produce and were often prone to rapid weathering, and until after World War II most railroads stuck with boxcar red. As better paints became available in the latter half of the century, however, all freight cars tended to become more colorful, almost to the point of becoming downright garish.

CARLOADS AND LCL

The boxcar was the universal freight car, and its use was affected by rules and rates. The favored customers were those with their own factory sidings who could completely fill a boxcar with each outbound load. There were some rules, however, established by the Interstate Commerce Commission, as to what cars could be loaded and where they could be directed (these rules applied to all general-service freight cars, not just boxcars). There were essentially two types of cars available for use: a "home" car belonging to the railroad itself or a "foreign" car belonging to another railroad. A third type of car, the "private owner" car, carried its own loading and use restrictions.

To keep interchanged cars moving, when a customer requested a car, the railroad's agent was obligated to first see if there was an empty foreign car available that could be routed in the direction of its home road. For example, the Chicago & Eastern Illinois might have a customer in Chicago with a load bound for California. The first preference for loading would be an empty belonging to the Santa Fe or another Western carrier, but certainly not a B&O or Florida East Coast car. If no foreign car was readily available, he could load a C&EI car and send it west. These rules applied to "general service" cars. Some cars belonging to private owners or equipped with special interior racks might be in "assigned service" with specific instructions for return routing when empty.

To keep a railroad's car from becoming a static warehouse when delivered to its destination, the customer was given three working days to unload the car before a daily "demurrage" fee was charged for holding the car. One advantage of privately owned cars or those in assigned service is that they could be used as mobile warehouses and not be hit with the demurrage charges if they were held at their destination until their cargoes were needed in the factory.

But not all cargoes were large enough to fill a boxcar. In the first 100 years of the railroad business, these "LCL" (Less-than-Carload Lot) customers were a major nuisance to the railroads. Being defined by law as "common carriers," the railroads were obligated to provide service to any customer, and the LCL business tended to be labor-intensive and often money-losing. Since the railroads had a rate structure based upon the value of the cargo and its weight, as well as its durability and potential for damage, they could not afford to tie up an entire car for a small load.

Thus the railroads set up transfer terminals in large cities and local freight houses in nearly every town. The railroad would then load numerous individual LCL shipments into one car and route it to a number of destinations, hopefully on a fairly

Like public timetables for their passenger trains, many railroads published freight schedule brochures for their freight customers. This one is from the New York Central was published in February 1954.
C. W. NEWTON COLLECTION

Before FedEx and UPS, the railroads would handle individual "Less than Carload Lot" (LCL) shipments. Here at a metropolitan freighthouse, LCL shipments are consolidated to make full carloads.
RAILFAN & RAILROAD COLLECTION

ABOVE: The Pennsylvania Railroad's long-held stance of internally standardizing its locomotive and car fleet resulted in the development of the X-29 steel boxcar. For much of the twentieth century, the PRR was one of America's largest and most-powerful railroads, and thousands of X-29s roamed North American rails. Many of these cars were outfitted with high-speed trucks, tightlock couplers, and steam lines (for train heating) for operation on passenger trains, as illustrated by this X-29 tucked between the E-unit and baggage car at the head end of Frisco's *Sunnyland* departing St. Louis in 1965.

ABOVE RIGHT: Major advances were made in the 1960s in the methods to brace loads inside boxcars to prevent shifting and damage while under way. Here, Missouri Pacific workers use "DF" (Damage Free) braces and wall brackets to secure a load of metal tanks. MISSOURI PACIFIC

RIGHT: High-cubic-foot-capacity boxcars, known as "Hi-Cubes," were developed for efficient transportation of large-size but low-density loads like automobile parts and home appliances. The Hi-Cubes typically have very large doors to permit loading by forklift trucks. The World War II-era railroads had to increase overhead clearances to new national standards to permit universal use of these cars, but by the late 1960s, they were becoming very popular. Here in 1963 a colorful Southern Pacific Hi-Cube was on an eastbound Chicago & North Western freight train at Dixon, Illinois. Compare the size to the adjacent typical steam-era 40-foot Lake Superior & Ishpeming boxcar.

logical route. Sensing the potential of the difference between the high LCL tariffs and lower carload rates, many "freight forwarders" entered the business with their own regional warehouses. These companies would solicit the smaller loads at the high rates and consolidate them into cars going to the destination warehouse, paying the railroad the lower carload rate. Even with the necessary handling, this was a potentially profitable business. It became even more effective in the 1920s when motor trucks could be used for local distribution, and the railroad cars could be kept for just the long haul between major terminals.

The U.S. Post Office and Railway Express Agency set up similar services for the even smaller shipments, but they generally used passenger trains, rather than freights, for faster service on predictable schedules. Some railroads introduced their own LCL service, such as the New York Central's "Pacemaker" and the Missouri Pacific's "Eagle Merchandise Service," which used special freight trains running on fast, published schedules.

THE MODERN BOXCAR

Throughout the 1960s, 1970s, and 1980s, boxcars continued to grow in size and sophistication. To prevent damage to fragile cargo, cars were built with cushion underframes and long-throw cushioned couplers. Standardized internal bracing, racks, and movable bulkheads were applied to secure the loads during transit and replace the nailed-in bracing of the wooden-interior era.

Before World War II, the boxcar had grown to 50 feet in length for lightweight but space-consuming cargos like lumber, automobiles, automobile assembly parts, furniture, and home appliances. By the 1960s the auto industry was building specialized plants in cities hundreds of miles apart. Frames from Kansas City and fenders from New Jersey might come together in Detroit to produce a new automobile that would be shipped to California. The railroads provided special freight cars for such movements, including mammoth 89-foot "High-Cube" (high cubic-foot capacity) cars to handle the relatively lightweight loads.

A quick scan of the road names on the cars in Conrail's Allentown Yard in Pennsylvania in 1979 reveals that much of the traffic relates to the paper mills in Maine and Canada. Kaolin clay for coating paper is shipped north in covered hoppers, while finished rolls of paper return south in boxcars. Note the yellow Railbox cars that can be sent anywhere and are exempt from the "return home" rule, as well as the blue "incentive per diem" shortline boxcars.

By the 1970s, the PS-1 40-footer, with its 50-ton capacity, had been replaced in popularity with the 50-foot, 77-ton capacity rib-side boxcar with a wide ten-foot sliding door to permit easy loading with a fork lift. These cars had "nailable" steel floors and hundreds of tie-down fixing points recessed into the walls. They could also be equipped with cushion underframes or cushion couplers and a variety of internal load-securing bulkheads or racks. Some cars were built with insulation for loads that needed a degree of protection from rapid temperature variations but not enough to require refrigeration or heating.

RAILBOX

By the early 1970s, the 40-foot boxcar fleet was aging, and the demand for the new 50-foot boxcars was growing so rapidly that a nationwide boxcar shortage was developing. One of the problems was utilization, where too many empties did not qualify for reloading under the "return toward home" ICC rules and spent too much time either moving empty or awaiting appropriate loads.

In 1973 a committee of rail executives set about to resolve the matter with a pool of new general-service boxcars that would be exempt from the "load toward home" rule. In late 1956 the Pennsylvania Railroad and Norfolk & Western joined with the Rail-Trailer Company of Chicago to create the TrailerTrain Company to establish the equipment and facilities for nationwide trailer-on-flatcar "piggyback" service to move highway trailers on flatcars. By 1970 nearly every other railroad in the country had bought into TrailerTrain, and it had done such a fine job with the piggyback business, that it was the logical vehicle to acquire and operate the new boxcar fleet.

Thus "Railbox" was created in January 1974 as a subsidiary of TrailerTrain, and before the end of the year the rapidly growing fleet of colorful yellow standard RBOX cars was hitting the rails. They carried the slogan, "Next Load, Any Road" and had very few restrictions on their routing, since they were considered home-road cars by every owner of TrailerTrain, which comprised almost the entire American rail network.

A study of the first two years' service by one of the first Railbox cars, RBOX 10013, showed that within 24 months it had traveled from coast to coast and border to border and just about everywhere in between. By its fifth birthday, RBOX 10013 had racked up over 100,00 miles.

By 1980 the Railbox fleet had grown to over 20,000 yellow boxcars of two standard designs: the original RBOX 50-footers with a single ten-foot sliding door on each side and the ABOX 50-footers with a six-foot plug door on each side in addition to the ten-foot slider, to provide a 16-foot loading opening where needed. The Railbox fleet was a great success and continues to produce the highest revenue-generating load ratio in the general-service car business.

The Railbox program was so successful that a similar "Railgon" program was inaugurated by TrailerTrain in 1979 that fielded a fleet of nearly 2,000 free-running black gondola cars, used mostly for loading of steel products. (The company rejected one suggestion that instead of "Next Load, Any Road," the GONX fleet should carry the slogan "Here Today, Gon Tomorrow.")

INCENTIVE PER-DIEM CARS

In another effort to resolve the same boxcar utilization problem of the early 1970s, the ICC introduced the "Incentive Per-Diem" program for certain high-quality boxcars. Per-diem is the "rent" one railroad pays for the use of another railroad's car. If the Santa Fe loaded one of its own cars in California, for example, in 1950 and sent it to New York City,

In the 1970s the railroad industry introduced the "Incentive Per Diem" program that gave higher rental rates to certain cars that were exempt from the "load toward home" rule, and many shortlines "sold" their reporting marks to boxcar leasing companies for a small profit at no cost. When business was strong, and the cars were running all over the country fully loaded, the system worked superbly. In the late 1970s, however, a recession caused business to plunge, and suddenly all the big roads wanted to get these high-rent cars off their lines and began to send them all home. The little Middletown & New Jersey was soon flooded with returning blue boxcars, and in January 1980 it had to open nearly five miles of its abandoned main line south of Slate Hill, New York, to store them. Here the M&NJ's two GE 44-ton diesels were laboring to stash the unwanted cars, a task made more difficult by the fact that the "run-around" track here at Slate Hill would hold only two boxcars at a time!

the car would travel "free" on Santa Fe tracks to Chicago, but once it was handed over to the New York Central, the NYC would pay a daily per-diem fee on that car until it was delivered to the customer and then returned, either loaded or empty, to another railroad. As long as it was on a different railroad, the Santa Fe would receive the per-diem rental. At that time the per-diem was calculated at midnight. The rent would be paid by whatever railroad the car was on at midnight.

This midnight accounting time resulted in the entire railroad industry focusing its operations on delivering interchange to connecting railroads before midnight, to stick the other guy with the per-diem fee. Stories are legendary about the "midnight shove," when both railroads would be scrambling to deliver its cars into the interchange before the magic midnight stroke—and crashing into each other in the middle of the same track!

All of this per-diem was kept track of by an army of clerks who would record the location of every car at midnight of every day. With the advent of computers, "incremental per-diem" accounting became practical, and the fees were charged based upon the actual time of interchange and not the car's location at midnight.

While per-diem fees could be substantial, most railroads simply canceled out what they owed each other, and very little cash actually changed hands. If the Santa Fe owed the NYC a $100 fee and the NYC owed the Santa Fe $110 in charges, the actual cash transaction would be just the $10 difference. This little technicality, however, could have an awesome impact on the entire industry if a major railroad went bankrupt, since the bankrupt railroad was not obligated to pay the per-diem debt, but the solvent interchange partner was (the bankrupt railroad just added the per-diem to its protected debt, while the solvent carrier had to pay cash to the bankrupt one). When the sprawling Penn Central went bankrupt in 1970, the per-diem deficits alone caused nearly every other railroad in the region to declare bankruptcy, as well, to keep from being bled of cash by the black hole of the PC. With both the interchange partners bankrupt, however, the per-diem debt-canceling process went right back to normal, again, just like between two solvents.

The Incentive Per-Diem (IPD) program of the 1970s was to improve car utilization by providing a fleet of new cars that, like Railbox, was exempt from the "load toward home" rule and that would have a higher-than-usual per diem rate to encourage its

Uncle Bob's Tariff

Alfred E. Perlman hated steam locomotives. As executive vice-president of the Denver & Rio Grande Western in 1950, he regarded them as money-burning relics of a gloomy past that should be swept away by the space-age efficiency of diesel power. Steam locomotives were not to be honored or preserved, but to be scrapped without emotion.

Bob Richardson had a very different opinion. "Uncle Bob" was a railfan and businessman who had started a small museum at his "Narrow Gauge Motel" in Alamosa, Colorado, that catered to railfans and tourists who visited that Mecca of the surviving narrow-gauge lines still operated by the D&RGW with steam locomotives. Richardson was also one of the more high-profile opponents of the D&RGW's efforts to abandon the narrow-gauge lines. Mr. Perlman disliked Bob Richardson almost as much as he disliked steam engines.

Under Perlman's orders, the Rio Grande's steam locomotives were being scrapped as rapidly as possible. On the neighboring Rio Grande Southern, however, were still a few intact gems, including the 346, a classic D&RGW 2-8-0 built by Baldwin in 1881. In 1947 it had been leased to the Montezuma Lumber Company for use on its five-mile line from the sawmill at McPhee to the RGS connection at Dolores.

Richardson bought the 346 for $800. The RGS was willing to pull it dead on its own wheels to Durango, but the D&RGW flatly refused to move the engine the 200 narrow-gauge miles from there over Cumbres Pass to Alamosa. As a common-carrier, the D&RGW was legally obligated to move the locomotive for a paying customer, but the basis for its refusal was a technicality: there was no published tariff freight rate for dead locomotives.

Richardson was stymied. The 346 sat in Dolores as he related the story to a visitor to his motel. Edward Mahoney was a steam fan, but he was also traffic manager for the Atomic Energy Commission and a former chief clerk for the Santa Fe. Mahoney had spent his entire career dealing with rates and tariffs and knew how the system functioned.

A few weeks later Richardson received in the mail the latest rate bulletins and a note to check a specific page. There on the new list was a temporary tariff for "hauling dead narrow gauge engines with a weight of less than 100,000 pounds from Durango to Alamosa" at a rate of $1.79 per mile. It turned out that Mahoney had used his long-term business relationship with his friend W. M. Carey, the D&RGW General Freight Agent. Mr. Carey quietly entered the tariff among others that he was presenting at a rate meeting of traffic agents.

Al Perlman never did figure out how that tariff got posted, and he departed the D&RGW to become president of the New York Central before any heads could roll (on the NYC, Perlman continued his anti-steam policy, which is why not a single example of the NYC's most famous passenger locomotive, the regal 4-6-4 Hudson, was ever preserved).

Bob Richardson got his narrow gauge 2-8-0 moved to Alamosa and displayed it for many years at his motel. In 1958 he and Cornelius Hauck established the Colorado Railroad Museum in Golden. By 1962 the 346 was overhauled and steamed at the Golden museum (above, in 1985), and it has been one of the premier attractions there ever since.

Prior to the 1960s, new automobiles were shipped in boxcars, and it was an inefficient and expensive process. Seeking a more cost-effective railcar for automobiles, they developed the open "auto-rack" multi-level flatcar. The same new clearance standards that permitted the Hi-Cube boxcars let the auto-rack grow to three levels. The Nickel Plate Road owned only three tri-level auto racks (built by Novi Car Company), but one of them is at Calumet, Illinois, in 1965, loaded with new Ford Mustangs.

Vandals quickly discovered that shiny new automobiles in open auto-racks were great targets for everything from thrown stones to shotgun blasts and were rolling parking lots for the theft of everything from radios to batteries to tires and complete engines. Thus, the trilevel auto rack soon got metal or fiberglass sides and tops and securely locked end doors. Here at a GM auto plant in Moraine, Ohio (just south of Dayton), auto-racks were being loaded in September 1989.
BRADLEY McCLELLAND

expedited movement. This concept got a cool reception from the big railroads, but venture capital groups saw the potential of the idea. There was only one hitch: the new rules applied only to railroad-owned cars. The money men, however, found a loophole. They bought the new cars and leased them to shortline railroads for about $300–$400 per month; and the railroads could earn about $600 a month on a $20-per-day per-diem fee, as long as the car was on a foreign railroad, which it nearly always was. In effect, the shortlines were renting their reporting marks to the boxcar owners. The spiffy new 50-footers were painted in colorful liveries with the shortline's name emblazoned in bold letters, just like the big guys!

As long as the economy was good and the boxcars kept rolling, the scheme worked extremely well. On the few occasions when a business recession slowed carloadings, the big carriers, eager to get the expensive IPD cars off their property, sent them home empty. Once on home rails, an IPD car stopped earning money, and some of the smaller shortlines actually had contracted for more boxcars than their entire railroad could hold! The five-mile-long Middletown & New Jersey actually had to "un-abandon" about three miles of derelict main line south of Slate Hill, New York, in 1980 to store one-third of its massive 600-car fleet of blue boxcars when they suddenly started coming home to roost.

RIGHT: Although experimentation was done as early as the 1920s, practical piggyback service got underway in the 1950s. Early trailer-on-flatcar technology was complex and time-consuming, as shown here on the Wabash at Welland Junction, Ontario, on August 1, 1957. All those chains and clamps to secure the trailer to the modified conventional flatcar had to be attached by hand. JIM SHAUGHNESSY

BELOW: The Seaboard Air Line set up a publicity photo north of Jacksonville, Florida, in 1960 with a new Alco RS11 and a train of its new piggyback trailers that grew into its "Razorback" service. The approaching streamliner appears to be the Silver Meteor. WARREN CALLOWAY COLLECTION

During the 1980s and 1990s, the Railbox and IPD fleets were rationalized to meet the normal traffic patterns and were an integral part of the American freight train scene as the twenty-first century arrived.

BEYOND THE BOXCAR

The 40-foot boxcar had long been a favorite for grain loading, because its 50-ton payload could be handled by almost any prairie branch line. While wooden "grain doors" remained a common loading device for keeping the grain inside the boxcar's sliding side doors, companies like Signor produced even more economical heavy paper grain doors with reinforcing straps that could be simply stapled over the inside of the door opening to retain the grain, which would be loaded from the elevator spout through the top of the door opening. With the upgrading of most branchline track to be able to handle modern 100-ton freight cars, covered hoppers became a much more convenient and economical way to transport grain. Long roof hatches made the load easier and quicker to distribute evenly inside the car, and the hopper bottoms made unloading much simpler than shoveling out the door by hand. By the 1990s, the use of boxcars for grain loading had almost completely ceased.

From the days of horse-and-buggy, railroads had provided special boxcars for transporting road vehicles, and the automobile in the 1920s was just another load for a boxcar. Unfortunately, an auto doesn't fit a boxcar very well, and even a number of automobiles with creative loading still waste a lot of space. One of the first "modern" freight cars designed to replace the boxcar for a specific load was the auto-rack, a long, two- or three-level flat-car which could carry a dozen or more automobiles. The first auto-racks of the 1960s had open sides, but vandalism quickly proved to be a temptation with the shiny new vehicles in plain view. The auto-racks were given lightweight metal or fiberglass sides, a roof and lockable end doors, and they were soon more kin to the time-honored boxcar than their genesis flatcar.

The very first rail freight was carried on a flatcar, and a hundred years later the flatcar posed a new threat to the boxcar. As early as the 1920s, some railroads had been experimenting with hauling highway trailers on flatcars, and in the

By the 1960s, it was becoming obvious that something better was needed for loading trailers than "circus" loading. In an effort to reduce weight by not carrying the truck's highway wheels, they developed the "Flexi-Van," which used a small pivot plate on the flatcar to permit the trailer to be backed onto the car from the side. This view from the early 1960s shows the Milwaukee Road's intermodal facility adjacent to its Milwaukee, Wisconsin, locomotive shop. This creative but mechanically complex system was rendered obsolete by the Piggy Packer and large straddle-cranes that would follow. MILWAUKEE ROAD, COURTESY JIM STAROSTA

1950s the Pennsylvania Railroad began to aggressively market its "TrucTrain" concept with both railroad-owned and private-carrier trailers. This TOFC (Trailer-On-Flat-Car) service was offered on special dedicated "piggyback" trains operating on fast regular schedules, like a passenger train. The rates were low enough that for anything over about 500 miles, it was cheaper for a trucking company to put its trailer on a flatcar instead of haul it over a highway with a tractor and a driver.

Prior to this, customers not located on a rail siding would have used the truck to carry the load to a freight house or team track to be loaded into a boxcar, but now the truck could run door-to-door without being unloaded and still take advantage of the more economical rail long-haul.

By the 1960s piggybacking was becoming a universal practice in railroading, and the service was greatly expanded as TrailerTrain invested in the new 89-foot flatcars that could handle two standard highway trailers. As ICC regulations permitted bigger and bigger highway trailers, the railroads scrambled to match each advance with a new wrinkle in flatcars.

The earliest piggyback loading was done "circus-style" with a ramp at the end of a stub track, and the trailer being backed aboard the flatcar from the end. Drop-down tire ramps at the ends of the flatcars permitted loading many cars on a single track from a single ramp—but the trailers could be loaded only one at a time, as the tractor had to "escape" after dropping each trailer. In the 1970s a mobile "Piggy Packer" was developed that could simply pick up an entire loaded trailer and deposit it on the flatcar from the side. Soon, large facilities were laid out using such machines, along with traveling cranes, to quickly load an entire train from the sides.

A drawback of the traditional TOFC format is that a highway trailer carries a lot of "dead" weight in its wheels and undercarriage. With the need for circus-loading eliminated, special "spine cars" were designed that reduced the weight of the flatcar and let the trailer ride closer to the rails, lowering its center of gravity. Whereas the older flats required the trailer to be manually chained in place, the newer cars used wheel wells and a power-locking "fifth wheel" to quickly secure the trailer to the car.

CONTAINERS AND DOUBLE-STACKS

American railroad ingenuity completely changed global commerce patterns when the double-stack articulated container car was developed in the 1980s. These cars were so simple and cost-effective that it was cheaper to unload a ship on one coast and "land-bridge" the cargo by train completely across the continent, rather than route the ship to the other coast via the Panama Canal. An excellent example is this westbound Union Pacific double-stacker crossing Clio viaduct near Portola, California, in June 1999 on the former Western Pacific line that traverses the Feather River Canyon. TOM KLINE

As rapid progress was being made in the piggy-back technology, this "intermodal" concept was being developed in worldwide ocean commerce. One of the biggest problems with sailing ships from the earliest days was the need to "break bulk" to load and unload cargoes one piece at a time. It was not only time-consuming, but it encouraged theft and damage. Part of the rapidly growing intermodal technology that grew out of the side-loading of trailers involved building trucks with the cargo "boxes" that could be lifted off the highway chassis, including the Flexi-Van, which used flatcars with small pivoting turntables on their frames to accept a van trailer from the side and swing it onto the flatcar (previous page).

This concept of the "box" quickly grew into the standard international shipping "container." A container on a truck chassis could be loaded, locked and sealed, driven to a railroad, transferred onto a flatcar, and transported to a seaport. The locked container could then be loaded aboard a ship, transported halfway across the world, and delivered by rail or highway to the intended receiver. The longshoremen and labor unions fought this viciously, as it would cost thousands of jobs, but the economic advantage of the container was irresistible.

At first the railroads handled the containers like wheelless trailers on flatcars, but then the container had to be manually secured to the deck. To make more efficient use of the standard universal container, the railroads soon developed a variety of "well cars" that held the containers without any additional locking device. Since these well cars could be made lower to the rails, it was possible to stack the containers two-high and still meet normal overhead clearances (which could not be done on a conventional flatcar deck). To maximize the load capacity and reduce weight, long articulated cars were developed that were made of five permanently connected segments, each of which could carry double-stacked containers (the containers were already designed to interlock when stacked one atop the other and were strong enough to be stacked quite high, depending on their loads). Each "platform" of these well cars was usually bottomless with just lugs large enough to hold the container, while the shallow car sides kept it securely in place with no need for further chains or locks.

These "double-stack" cars were so efficient and economical that it became cheaper to carry a container across the continent by rail than it was to keep it aboard ship and route it around via the Panama Canal to an East Coast port, as would have been done in the break-bulk days. Huge and fast specially designed container ships would depart the Orient and run a great circle route across the Pacific Ocean to North America, usually making landfall in the Pacific Northwest. Containers bound for the East Coast would be unloaded at harbors from Vancouver and Tacoma south to Los Angeles and routed by train directly across the country. While most of the containers would be bound for customers in the U.S., some would then be loaded onto ships again on the East Coast for transport to Europe, in a concept known as the "land bridge" over North America. Since container ships become faster and more efficient as they get larger, many of the newer ships are "post-Panamax" designs which are much too big to fit through the Panama Canal. Their very existence is based on the success of the American double-stack container train.

And what is carried in those containers? Good ol' "boxcar business." Everything from household appliances and clothing to food and automobiles. A container is essentially the universal boxcar of the twenty-first century. A double-stacker looks a lot different from a string of "high cars" rolling across the prairies behind a steam locomotive, but the job it does is exactly the same.

The RoadRailer is a concept that dates back to the 1960s but did not gain commercial acceptance until the 1990s. The RoadRailer simply places railroad wheelsets beneath the back end of each trailer and eliminates the flatcar completely. Norfolk Southern saw the potential of the RoadRailer and invested heavily in perfecting the technology before introducing its "Triple Crown" service between specific markets. On September 24, 1995, Norfolk Southern RoadRailer 263 was passing through Cincinnati behind a lone GP60. BRADLEY McCLELLAND

A Chessie System grain train sweeps through amber waves of grain (in this case, corn) at Meyersdale, Pennsylvania, in late summer 1979. The train is moving westbound along the Baltimore & Ohio Railroad's Baltimore/Washington–Chicago main line. North American farmers grow the food, but railroads move both raw food—today, mostly grain in covered hoppers—and refined food to processing plants and finally to market. *MIKE SCHAFER*

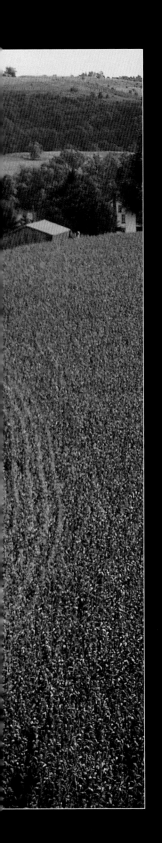

8

Food
on the Move

When the Pilgrims landed on Plymouth Rock, they found that the New World looked and felt a lot like the old one. The climate was like that of England, with cold winters and warm summers. The Indians taught them to plant corn, but other than that, the crops, game, and livestock were quite similar to that of the British Isles and Europe. Crops had to be planted in the spring, grown in the summer, harvested in the fall, and stashed away

In the summer of 1976, the Canadian Pacific was still using traditional stock cars. Although classic in appearance, these are fairly modern double-deckers. The white lime wash was used to keep the floors reasonably sterile beneath the straw beds and to minimize the odors. Two loads and two empties are being lined up at Lambton Yard on the northwest side of Toronto for transfer to Agincourt Yard across town.

ABOVE: Stockyards were once common along the railroads in farm country. In April 1971 Burlington Northern's westbound Empire Builder barrels under the Illinois Central and past the stockyard at Polo, Illinois. Note how the pens are arranged alongside the corridor that leads to the loading ramp.

RIGHT: Livestock being shipped long distances had to taken out of the cars at regular intervals for exercise and feeding. Since this required "drovers" to herd the cattle off and back on, they often traveled with the shipment. Some railroads built larger-than-normal "drovers cabooses," like this wooden Cotton Belt classic that had been preserved on the Graysonia, Nashville & Ashdown Railroad in Arkansas in 1989.

for a long, cold winter. Even urban dwellers kept chickens, pigs, and a cow or two in the back yard. They could not have imagined herds of buffalo as far as the eye could see or wheatfields larger than some countries or sweeping valleys full of citrus orchards beneath the endless summer sun of Southern California. But the American continent offered all of that with a range of geography and climate that would stagger the imagination. Folks would just have to walk 3,000 miles to take advantage of it all.

As the railroads spread westward in the mid-1800s, Americans began to exploit the inherent advantages of each region and climate. The Midwest had rich farmland, while the Western plains were ideal for raising cattle. Fruits and vegetables could be grown all year around in the South and Southwest. The Civil War of the 1860s both interrupted and propelled westward expansion, and as railroads spread across the country, they sold land and brought in immigrants to populate it. Most of the pioneers found they could make a lot more money in farming or the cattle business than they could by digging for the elusive California gold.

From the beginning of time, the easiest way to keep meat fresh was to keep it alive until it was time to eat it, and most livestock was raised close to the consuming market. But cattle need space to graze, and the valuable farmland near the Eastern cities was much more productive if planted with grains or vegetables. The vast expanses of the Great Plains that had supported the buffalo herds were ideal for beef cattle, and rail transportation in the 1870s made it accessible to the entire nation. The legends of the cowboys and "Wild West" were created from the cattle business that kept the population "Back East" supplied with T-bones.

Cattle thrived on the open range land, and the differences in climate between the Montana high country and the Texas plains could be utilized to maximize the yield. Cattle from warm Texas breeding ranches could be moved to Montana for summer grazing and then to Iowa feedlots for fattening for market and a final trip to the slaughterhouse.

Although railroads had carried livestock in open cars on a limited basis for many years, the true "stock car" didn't develop until the 1860s. In general, it looked like a boxcar with horizontal slats instead of solid sides. The opening of the Chicago Union Stockyards in 1865 prompted the rapid development of similar facilities throughout the Midwest and Eastern Seaboard, and stockcar fleets grew rapidly.

Handling cattle, however, was not a simple matter, because the living animals had to be fed and watered and protected from injury and sickness that would damage their market value. This meant that huge lineside stockpens had to be built that could handle entire trainloads of livestock for exercise, food, and water. And since cattle are seldom smart enough to get off the train by themselves, movements were accompanied by cowboy "drovers" to load and unload them (some railroads would put a passenger car or oversized "drovers caboose" on a stock train for the men to ride in). In 1873, Federal legislation was passed that mandated that cattle had to be unloaded after 28 hours for a minimum of five hours rest in a lineside pen. Thus, longer journeys became more time-consuming and expensive. As time went on, stock cars equipped for feed and water could be used to extend the time stock could be kept in the cars. Although most rail moves involved livestock being transported to their doom in a slaughterhouse, humane treatment en route was not just a moral matter but a practical one, since starved, sick, or injured stock was of substantially reduced value to the customer.

In the 1870s, the advent of refrigeration encouraged meat wholesalers to change their approach from transporting live cattle across the entire country to moving dressed meat. Large slaughterhouses and packing plants were established in places like Iowa and Missouri, and the meat went to market in ice-cooled refrigerator cars. Until the mid-twentieth century, the cattle business settled down to using stock cars for moving live cattle on relatively short hauls from ranches to feedlots to packing houses and then as processed meat in refrigerator cars to the wholesale distributors.

As motor trucks grew in size and reliability, the inherently small-scale cattle moves shifted to truck transport.

CONRAIL AND "HAMTRAK"

One of the last regular moves of cattle on an American main line was actually into New Jersey—not exactly cattle-drive country, but very typical of the receiving end of many livestock movements. In 1988, Conrail was moving about six carloads a week from Chicago to the Linden Packing Company in Newark, New Jersey. Although the concept was identical, this move looked quite different from the Rio Grande out of Parlin, Colorado. Instead of wooden stock cars

continued on page 119

The Last Roundup

On September 11, 1953, cowboys were driving their herd of Mexican longhorns across the narrow-gauge track at Parlin, Colorado, as Denver & Rio Grande Western 2-8-2 483 rambled into town from Gunnison. ALL PHOTOS, JOHN KRAUSE

On the previous day, the 483 had come over from Salida with some of the empty stock cars for the 40-car train that would be loaded at Parlin on September 11. Engine 480 had run ahead with just a caboose so that its crew could get into Gunnison earlier and get its 8-hour rest to be available early the next morning to run to Parlin and begin the loading.

In the 1880s, the predecessors of the Denver & Rio Grande Western were reaching south and westward from Denver into the heart of the Rocky Mountains with a network of three-foot narrow-gauge lines to tap the silver and coal mines of the region as they reached toward Salt Lake City, Utah. After negotiating the spectacular Royal Gorge west of Pueblo, Colorado, the main line turned west at Salida, climbed over Marshall Pass, and picked up the Black Canyon of the Gunnison River to reach Montrose and Grand Junction, Colorado, and Salt Lake City. In the early 1890s, however, the Royal Gorge line was converted to standard gauge, and the Marshall Pass line was completely bypassed by a new standard-gauge main line to the north via Leadville and Glenwood Springs.

About that same time, however, more narrow-gauge lines were built to the south, linking Alamosa, Durango, and Silverton, and these were ultimately connected by the Rio Grande Southern between Durango and Montrose to create what became known as the "Narrow Gauge Circle" with 515 miles of main line. This rugged little system became the economic backbone of the region, bringing in merchandise and building supplies and taking out ore, coal, oil, and agricultural products. During World War II, the narrow gauge even carried uranium for the top-secret nuclear weapons program.

The arid valleys of the high country made fine cattle grazing land, and stock trains became a seasonal tradition on the narrow gauge, for which the Rio Grande had amassed a sizable fleet of stock cars. By the 1950s, however, motor trucks were reaching into the area, and the narrow-gauge lines were being abandoned as their revenue sources dried up. The Marshall Pass line had been abandoned west of Sapinero in 1949, and the lines around Gunnison saw infrequent moves to service the Colorado Fuel &

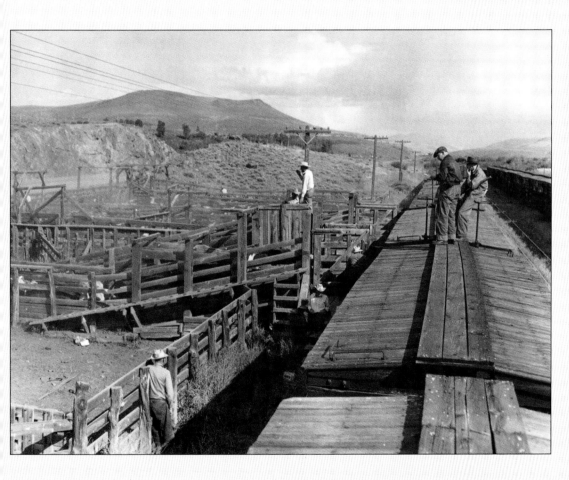

The "stemwinder" handbrakes on the top of the cars not only created an image of "old time" railroading, they also provided a nice stool where the brakeman could sit while waiting for each car to be loaded. Note the traditional wooden brake club under arm of one of the brakemen. Although this train is equipped with air brakes, the brakemen would "tie down" the handbrake for safety as each car was spotted for loading.

It was a scene right out of a "Marlboro Country" cigarette ad as tomorrow's Steak 'n' Shake Steakburgers were being herded aboard the narrow-gauge stock cars by cowboys in weatherbeaten hats.

Iron coal mine at Crested Butte and a handful of local customers, including some cattle pens.

On September 10, 1953, a D&RGW 2-8-0 ventured west from Gunnison to gather some stock cars from Sapinero, and two big 2-8-2s came over from Salida. The next day a 40-car stock "Extra" (a non-scheduled train) was at the cattle pen at Parlin as cowboys on horseback drove in a herd of Mexican longhorns for shipment to Denver. It was a scene right out of John Wayne movie, but the work was real, and the movement was all business, carefully coordinated so that the locomotives and crews would be on hand at the right place and right time to move the trainload of cattle over

Marshall Pass to the stockpens at the end of the narrow gauge at Salida. There, the cattle would be transferred to standard-gauge cars. As the train was loaded, two more locomotives came over Marshall Pass to work as helper engines for the eastbound climb with the loaded train.

By the end of the day, the last roundup at Parlin was complete, and 40 loads of cattle were bound for Denver in the time-honored manner with four plumes of coal smoke reaching into the evening sky out of Sargent, and the lusty exhausts of the 2-8-2s filling the valley with their sound. A month later, the final stock train on the Marshall Pass line carried the Powderhorn Roundup out of Iola and into the history books.

With Mikados 483 and 480 on the front and 485 and 489 working as pushers 30 cars back, the 40-car "Stock Extra" departs Parlin for the climb over Marshall Pass in the late afternoon of September 11, 1953. By union agreement, the only trains over Marshall Pass that were permitted four locomotives were livestock moves. Remarkably, two of these engines steam today—the 480 on the Durango & Silverton Narrow Gauge and the 489 on the Cumbres & Toltec Scenic Railroad.

One of the last regular railroad cattle moves in the U.S. was run for Linden Packing of Newark, New Jersey, by Conrail, which handled two carloads three days a week from Chicago to Newark over the former Pennsylvania Railroad. Here during the summer of 1985 at Jacks Tower in Jacks Narrows, near Mt. Union, Pennsylvania, Conrail piggybacker TV-12 is carrying two of the Linden steel double-deck 91-foot stock cars.

Continued from page 115

dating back to the 1890s, the Linden Packing moves were in huge, 91-foot-long, double-decked, steel cars. The stock was considered a "regular" move on Conrail, departing as two-car blocks three days a week. They would load at 47th Street in Chicago in the evening and be expedited eastward as the first cars on the fast piggyback (trailer-on-flatcar intermodal) train TV-12. Upon arrival at the former-Lehigh Valley Oak Island Yard, the cars would be immediately moved to the Linden Packing stockpen at the "Stock Switch" track in Newark.

Although the Linden cattle move ended in 1989, another extensive livestock move continues on the Union Pacific for the Clougherty Packing Company of Los Angeles—though it involves hogs rather than steers. Clougherty produces a widely distributed pork sausage under the brand name "Farmer John," and for this high-volume business, it gathers hogs from pens along the Union Pacific in Missouri, Kansas, Nebraska, and Colorado. In 1989 the traditional 45-foot triple-deck, wood-sided stock cars carrying 200 hogs were replaced with new 60-foot steel Gunderson cars that carry 300, but the basic operating pattern remained unchanged. The stock cars would be gathered at the various originating pens and sent westward to North Platte, Nebraska, where they would be grouped together in one "block" on the UP's fast symbol freight SLOAZ (St. Louis–Oakland Trailers), which thus became a "piggybacker" in more ways than one!

At Cheyenne, cars from Gill, Colorado, would be added, and the hog block would continue westward to Salt Lake City, where it would be switched to the CSLAZ (Chicago–Los Angeles Trailers) for the run southwest to L.A. En route, the UP has set up watering facilities on the main line, where the hogs are showered down inside the cars without ever being removed from the train. Upon arrival in L.A.'s East Yard, the hog cars would be met by a switch engine, which would take them immediately to the Farmer John plant for unloading.

Sixty-foot steel Gunderson stock cars are being loaded at trackside pens in Nebraska as cattlemen take a break from their work to watch a Union Pacific passenger special fly by on the Omaha–Ogden main line in 1990. The cars can carry up to 300 hogs; the cars' louvered car sides can be adjusted to let in light and air while keeping out rain or snow.

In 1971, this classic Chicago & North Western wooden refrigerator car was spending its last days as a storage shed for ice used in locomotive water coolers and caboose "ice boxes" in the Penn Central's former-New Haven engine terminal at Maybrook, New York. Note the stemwinder handbrake and steel underframe construction.

This entire Farmer John operation became unofficially known as "Hamtrak," and it was not without its interesting moments. Author David Lustig told the following tale in the September 1988 issue of *Railfan & Railroad* Magazine from a UP crew member in the 45-foot car days:

"The only real difficulty we've had is that occasionally a door will come open on the road. That happened a while back, and nearly a whole carload of hogs stepped off into the darkness at 70 miles per hour. We scattered hogs over most of a division. When the train got to Salt Lake City, they called the conductor on the carpet for not spotting the problem sooner. He had been riding in the caboose and defended himself by relating that the stock was blocked near the front of the train, it

was night, and 'them things don't make no sparks when they hit the ground!'"

Movements like Linden and Farmer John were once commonplace, but livestock is one of the few major commodities that have left the rails almost totally. And by the mid-twentieth century, the railroads were quite happy to see that particularly troublesome business go to the highway—or more preferably, into a local packing house and be shipped out in refrigerator cars as packaged meat.

REFRIGERATOR CARS

America's railroads have one of the best refrigerator-car services in the world. The nation's desire for fresh meat and produce gave the railroads a ready market for refrigerated transit as

early as the 1880s, but the equipment required was expensive for the time—a new refrigerator car cost almost twice as much as a boxcar—and it required specialized maintenance and inspection facilities such as icing stations. The early "reefers" (the common railroad name for refrigerator cars) were essentially heavily insulated boxcars with internal bunkers for carrying ice for cooling.

Although mechanical refrigeration was developed in the 1830s—about the same time as the earliest steam locomotives—the reciprocating compressors had to be powered by waterwheels or steam and were impractical for use in a railroad car. It was common practice to harvest ice from

ponds in the winter and store it in heavily insulated warehouses in quantities sufficient to last an entire summer and autumn. Later, stationary steam- or electric-powered ice-making plants could supply warehouses and refrigerator car bunkers with manmade ice. Because of the seasonal character of both the meat-packing and fresh produce businesses, however, much of this expensive equipment would be used only during the harvest season, setting idle the rest of the year.

Because of this, railroads were slow to invest in the new and unproven business. To resolve this problem, some of the bigger meat-packing companies purchased their own car fleets and built

Mechanized icing platforms like this one on The Milwaukee Road at Othello, Washington, in the 1950s were the leading edge of the trailing-edge of technology. Note the presence of both steel and wood-sheathed cars. By the 1970s, mechanical refrigerators would completely replace the iced reefers and render this complex obsolete and unused. Othello was the east end of the Milwaukee's Cascade electrification with wires extending west to Tacoma and Seattle. MILWAUKEE ROAD HISTORICAL ASSOCIATION ARCHIVES

121

ABOVE: The term "meat train" meant big business for the railroads and implied the best motive power and fastest schedules. Here on May 17, 1957, Nickel Plate 2-8-4 735 accelerates a meat train of Armour freezers over the Conneaut Creek Viaduct departing Conneaut, Ohio, to begin the final sprint of its journey from Chicago to Buffalo. JIM SHAUGHNESSY

RIGHT: Dressed meat for the wholesalers and delis of New York City were delivered into the heart of Manhattan by the New York Central's electrified West Side Freight Line. Morrell freezers from Iowa (leased from the North American Car Corporation) are being lined up for delivery to the nearby distributors in this view looking north at the 44th Street overpass in March 1963. Today this meat business is all handled by highway trucks, and the Freight Line at this point is now used by Amtrak to get from Penn Station to the former-NYC main line up the Hudson River to Albany. BOB HART SR.

their own icing stations. These "private car" operators worked out agreements with the railroads to haul the cars for a flat mileage rate.

This arrangement worked well, and by 1900 there were dozens of private fleets serving this fast-growing and highly competitive business. The largest of these was Armour, and with a fleet of 12,000 cars, it enjoyed a virtual monopoly on the refrigerator-car business and used its fleet to transport most of the produce as well. Between 1910 and 1920, however, antitrust legislation forced Armour and some of the other operators to sell out.

About this time, the railroads were seeing the advantage of getting into this lucrative market themselves. To better utilize a fleet of cars, several railroads would join forces and form their own "car line." The cars could then be used over a bigger geographic area on parts of each member's system as the harvests came in. For example Union Pacific, Southern Pacific, and Western Pacific comprised Pacific Fruit Express. PFE claimed its cars "followed the sun" by handling potatoes in the Pacific Northwest during the autumn, transporting California's citrus during the winter, and then moving spring fruit from the Southwest. PFE's bright orange cars could be seen almost anywhere, and sometimes entire trains were made of PFE reefers. These "fruit blocks" were high-priority trains and were often operated at passenger-train speeds, stopping only for crew changes and re-icing.

Throughout the first half of the twentieth century, colorful orange and yellow "meat trains" and "fruit blocks" were the fastest freights in the land. Cattle from the prairies would get a relatively short ride in a stockcar to the Midwestern packing plants and finish their journeys as dressed meat in refrigerator cars. Fruits and vegetables that could be harvested in overlapping seasons from the widely scattered regions of the West Coast and Deep South kept the wintry North in fresh produce all year around, thanks to refrigerator cars.

Mechanical reefers

If the cars and their contents were pre-cooled before loading, the initial load of three tons of ice would keep the car cold to its destination, and no re-icing stops would be needed. But in the 1940s, the food industry began exploiting the marketability of frozen products, and the technology demanded a change in transport. Enroute icing stops were needed for cars carrying frozen food, and salt had to be added to the ice to get the lower temperatures required to keep the cargo not just cold, but hard frozen.

One of the first big frozen commodities to gain widespread popularity was orange juice. It was impractical to use the ice cars to transport frozen juice concentrates because it was impossible to maintain the temperature needed—around 0 degrees Fahrenheit. To protect this business, PFE would have to replace some of its fleet with mechanically refrigerated cars.

By the late 1940s, reliable diesel-driven compressors had been developed that could be "packaged" as a modular units for use in refrigerator

Pacific Fruit Express was a joint venture between the Union Pacific and Southern Pacific (note both heralds). This 40-foot steel reefer with end ice bunkers was retired in the 1970s and preserved at the California State Railroad Museum.
TOM KLINE

ABOVE: A westbound Southern Pacific freight winding upgrade toward Donner Pass and past Donner Lake has a block of mechanical reefers in tow belonging to Fruit Grower's Express and SP's Pacific Fruit Express. Don't let the snow fool you; its June 1993.

LEFT: The Bangor & Aroostook was famous for handling Maine's massive potato crops each year in insulated boxcars and reefers. In this insider's point-of-view from 1976, pallets of bagged spuds are being transloaded from the reefers into the pier warehouse at Searsport, Maine, in preparation for being loaded onto the German cargo ship Anona for export to Dunkirk, France. After one disastrous winter in the early 1970s when entire trainloads of Maine potatoes spoiled en route when they were delayed for weeks on the bankrupt Penn Central, the rail interchange of potatoes off the BAR ceased completely.

cars. They carried their own fuel supply and could be easily monitored en route. They didn't need to be iced along the way and could easily maintain the temperature needed for frozen food.

In the 1950s, frozen food and juice were fast becoming a large part of PFE's business, and the company's mechanical car purchases increased rapidly. By 1970 the PFE fleet numbered over 12,000 cars, in spite of the fact that each car cost ten times more than a conventional iced reefer. But the mechanical cars didn't need icing stations, an expense PFE could do without. The last of the old ice cars surrendered to the scrappers in 1972.

About this time PFE was dealt a blow from truckers using the new federally funded Interstate highway system. PFE's market share began to seriously erode, and in 1978 it was decommissioned as a joint railroad company. The car fleet was equally divided between UP and SP, since the WP had bowed out in 1967. Each road used its smaller fleet for the remaining on-line shippers. Southern Pacific kept the PFE name, but a colorful era in American railroading had ended.

Back when Armour divested of a major portion of its car line assets, a partnership of several Eastern roads took over these operations under the banner of Fruit Growers Express, which was incorporated in 1920 to serve Southern and Eastern shippers. By 1926, Burlington and Great Northern had joined, giving FGE access to Midwest and Western markets as well.

By 1936 FGE's fleet totaled 26,327 cars, mostly ice refrigerator cars for produce traffic. Through its subsidiary National Car Company, FGE supplied

Frozen-food technology spelled the end for the simple but effective iced refrigerator car, since ice could not maintain the zero-degree temperature necessary for frozen products. Compact diesel-powered refrigeration units in the new mechanical reefers made the shipment of frozen food practical. One of the first companies to make extensive use of mechanical reefers was Tropicana, which now dispatches numerous trainloads of frozen orange juice from Florida to New Jersey and the Midwest in its own fleet of distinctive cars. Here in 1986, the Tropicana juice train highballs through Potomac Creek, Virginia, on the Richmond, Fredericksburg & Potomac. MIKE SCHAFER

Want some cereal to go with that orange juice? The railroads make that possible, too, by collecting the grain harvests from all across the country. Here in the summer of 1996, Union Pacific's former-Chicago & North Western Troy Grove branch local is at Rollo, Illinois, heading back to De Kalb and West Chicago. Note how old and new grain elevators have been combined into one complex. When the wooden elevators were built, grain was shipped out in boxcars, but now with the track upgraded, 100-ton covered hoppers are preferred. MIKE SCHAFER

cars for dairy and meat-packing houses, as well. By 1950 FGE had grown to 19 member railroads and was supplying cars to produce shippers all over the country, as well as meat packers like Rath, Kahns, and Oscar Mayer.

As with PFE, changes came in the 1950s with the conversion to mechanical reefers and competition from the Interstate highway system. FGE bought new equipment and went after additional business. In 1960, refrigerated truck trailers were purchased for piggyback service. By 1970 FGE was serving 60 different railroads, but carloadings continued to slide. In 1976 they were down to 41,045 from a high 30 years earlier of over 300,000. Some down-sizing was in order. More piggyback trailers were purchased, and the car fleet was trimmed to 14,000 cars, but most of these were insulated boxcars.

Carloadings began increasing again in the 1980s, making Fruit Growers Express one of the last of the old refrigerator-car operators remaining in business. Railroads still move a lot of chilled and frozen food, but now it is carried mostly in refrigerated truck trailers on piggyback flatcars or in refrigerated containers rather than refrigerator cars.

OUR DAILY BREAD

Formula for a McDonald's Big Mac: two all-beef patties, special sauce, lettuce, cheese, pickles, and onions (all delivered in mechanical reefers) on a sesame seed bun (made from flour which is made of grain, delivered in a covered hopper). The "amber waves of grain" of America's heartland that feed the nation and the world nowadays move in 110-ton covered hoppers from grain elevators on the prairies to flour mills scattered all across the country.

The ConAgra flour mill tucked in the Delaware River valley at Martin's Creek, Pennsylvania, for example, sends bulk flour out by truck to bread bakeries in the densely populated area between

The Piedmont Milling Company in Richmond, Virginia, is a fascinating small facility that makes animal feed and baking flour. Here in August 1982 it receives grain in 100-ton covered hoppers.

New York and Philadelphia. Utilizing the huge silos of a former cement plant, ConAgra receives grain in 110-ton covered hoppers from North Dakota.

Each kernel of wheat can yield five different food products, ranging from pure white flour to cattle feed made from the husk. This wheatfield-to-breadbasket business has belonged to the railroads since the B&O's first four-wheel "flour cars" of the 1830s, and it continues to thrive today.

Railroads are ideal for handling bulk grains, from wheat to corn to soybeans, and they made possible the vast distribution of the product. For more than a century, farmers would bring their crops by horse-drawn wagon or pickup truck into local grain elevators for sale and shipment to mills all across the country—and to export piers for shipment by sea to hungry nations throughout the world.

Grain was originally boxcar business, but by the 1960s it was moving sharply toward covered hoppers, instead. Hoppers were easier to load and particularly easier to unload, and by the 1980s the huge center-flow cars (with no center sill to obstruct the hopper bays) began to dominate the business. They could be built with round or flat sides and a variety of bottom bay patterns, but all proved to be efficient and economical for transporting grains in a safe and dry environment.

It is ironic that the Martin's Creek plant site that once shipped bulk cement out in covered hoppers now receives grain in updated versions of those same cars. Therein lies one of the great advantages of the railroad: its ability to adapt standard equipment to a wide variety of specific loads. In the case of covered hoppers, this could range from grain to cement to plastic pellets.

Grain trains are on the move on Union Pacific's Sherman Hill at Dale Junction, Wyoming, in 1990 as a train with MPI lease-fleet units met an opposing train with UP power. This grain could be moving to anywhere in the country to be made into everything from bread to pizza dough or buns for that Steak 'n' Shake Steakburger. TOM KLINE

America survives on liquid fuels and plastic products that are created from potentially hazardous chemicals. To support this way of life, large quantities of these liquids must be moved from place to place, and the railroads are the safest and most flexible means to do it. In September 1997, petroleum tanks were westbound in a Conrail freight, with pusher diesels on the rear, climbing Horseshoe Curve in Pennsylvania.

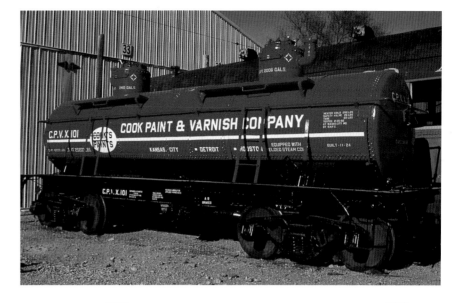

9 Petrochemicals
for Plasticville, U.S.A

Plastic pellets in covered hoppers. Now there's a commodity that they didn't anticipate on the Mad River & Lake Erie in 1838, when the first covered hopper was introduced for carrying grain. The entire petroleum and chemical industry that generates so much traffic for today's railroads did not come into being until Colonel Edwin L. Drake got the first crude oil out of his well at Titusville, Pennsylvania, on August 27, 1859.

This colorful Cook Paint & Varnish twin-dome tank car is a fine example of steam-era tank-car design. Each dome indicates a separate internal compartment. This non-insulated and non-pressurized car has its tank body riding on a heavy underframe. It was photographed in 1999 at the Illinois Railway Museum in Union, Illinois.

The first tank car in the U.S. was manufactured by American Car & Foundry in 1865 and is now on display at its plant in Berwick, Pennsylvania. It is essentially a four-wheel flatcar carrying two wooden barrels. The entire oil industry got its start in 1859 at Titusville in western Pennsylvania when Col. Edwin Drake sunk his first well. MIKE DEL VECCHIO

Until that time, railroads transported liquid products—from whale oil to molasses to wine—in barrels that could be loaded in gondolas, boxcars, and even stock cars. In the early 1860s, as Col. Drake's oil patch was beginning to pump the black crude faster than they could store it, the 42-gallon wooden barrel was the standard container for both transportation and measurement. Conventional railroad cars could be loaded with other commodities for "back hauls," even if that meant simply returning the empty barrels.

Even though the barrel system was inherently inefficient and labor-intensive, the railroads were reluctant to invest in "oil cars" that were unsuit-

able for other loading on the back haul and had to return empty. The oil companies, however, were eager to develop a better type of railroad car. Ironically, it took considerable bizarre experimentation to come up with a liquid-carrying freight car in light of the fact that nearly every steam locomotive was already accompanied by a tender that was two-thirds water tank! (The answer was cost, as none of the expensive locomotive tenders ever got interchanged to another railroad.)

After experimenting initially with open-top wooden vats on flatcars, by the 1870s the railroads and oil companies had found the basic design formula for the tank car that survives to this day: a

Because oil was essentially a one-way haul with little opportunity for a return-home load, early railroads were reluctant to invest in expensive tank cars that would be earning load revenues only half the time. This "Improved Combination Merchandise and Oil Car" was an attempt by the Overland Oil & Transportation Company to create a car that could provide a profitable return haul. To this day, most tank cars are privately owned through lease fleets. RAILFAN & RAILROAD COLLECTION

horizontal metal tank with internal baffles to reduce surging of the liquid in transit and a dome on the top for potential expansion of the load. The earliest of these were simply horizontal iron tanks mounted atop flatcars. The metal or wooden underframes extended beyond the end of the tanks to provide collision protection of the tank itself. Most cars had a slight taper to the bottom to permit draining of the full load through a discharge valve and outlet at the lowest point.

As the tank car grew in size and utility over the next decades, and construction went from iron to steel, the basic design and size remained fairly consistent. Since the railroads themselves were reluctant to invest in such special-use cars, the oil companies and shippers organized their own car fleets, very similar to what was being done with refrigerator cars. Tank cars were designed and built for specific products and shipping needs. Some cars had more than one internal compartment, so more than one type of oil or product could be shipped at the same time. It was easy to spot such a multiple-compartment car, as each compartment had its own expansion dome and bottom discharge connection. Two- and three-dome cars were not uncommon, and some tank cars came with as many as six compartments and domes.

It was not good practice to load a petroleum tank car with food oil, even after the interior had

been steam cleaned, so tank cars continued to be built for specialized loads. Special linings were applied to the tanks, from copper to rubber to glass, to provide the proper environment for the specific product being carried. The variety and quantity of things carried in tank cars grew as the availability of low-cost liquid transport encouraged customers to develop new uses for not only

The 23-mile Reader Railroad made a good living hauling trainloads of asphalt-grade crude oil from Waterloo, Arkansas, to the Missouri Pacific connection at Reader, Arkansas. In 1971 the Reader was still operating with three steam locomotives. Here, ex-U.S. Army 2-8-0 1702 gathers the tank cars at the Waterloo loading facility. The environmentalists had yet to discover the La Brea Tar Pit wonders of this garden spot of rural Arkansas.

A fuel dealer at Peace Dale, Rhode Island, is being served by the Narragansett Pier Railroad in May 1986. Thousands of small facilities like this are scattered all across the country. The fuel brought in by rail is then stored and shipped out by truck to home-heating customers or retail gas stations. Most people never realize that they are running their automobiles or heating their homes with fuel that was delivered by a railroad.

More than any war before in history, World War II was fought with gasoline. Here in a wartime publicity photo from Standard Oil, tank cars are being loaded with 100-octane aviation gasoline from storage tanks. RAILFAN & RAILROAD *COLLECTION*

coastal waterways, as ships and barges were an economical way to move the refined product to the heavily populated markets on the seacoasts or inland rivers.

At the turn of the twentieth century, the technology of the chemical industry was growing rapidly, and some of the products being created and shipped could be dangerous and even life-threatening in case of an accident. In 1903 the American Railway Association and Master Car Builders Association joined in issuing manufacturing specifications for tank cars that were used in interchange service. These specs were upgraded and expanded over the years under both industry and federal government (specifically, the Interstate Commerce Commission) overview to produce a fleet of safe and standardized tank cars.

WARTIME AND PLASTIC

With the onset of World War II, the railroads had to respond to a huge new influx of traffic when Nazi submarines began sinking the coastal oil tankers within sight of American beaches. U-boats could not torpedo a freight train, and soon mile-long trains of tank cars began replacing the ships on the refinery-to-market movement of fuel oil and gasoline.

Meanwhile, down in Elizabethton, Tennessee, a factory had been built on the East Tennessee & Western North Carolina Railroad to produce a new synthetic fiber called "rayon" that was used to make military parachutes. The "Tweetsie" was soon busy handling the inbound coal for the rayon mill's power plant and outbound fabric loads in boxcars to the Southern Railway and Clinchfield interchanges at Johnson City, Tennessee.

This was one of the first industrial installations of what would grow into the "petrochemical" industry, as the new technology of plastic began to reshape the face of America. Plastics had their beginning in 1909 with the creation of Bakelite, a rather brittle but useful material produced through a mixing of chemicals to produce long molecular chains with properties and textures not found in nature. Once the chemical processes were understood, an entirely new field of manmade materials began to develop in the late 1930s with the creation of nylon and urethane materials.

Following the war, the industry exploded in productivity and creativity with the development of vinyl resins, as well as acrylic and fiberglass. These materials could be turned into all sorts of

petroleum but the liquid byproducts of the slaughterhouses and other industrial processes. The railroads not only hauled crude oil to the refineries, but they then carried the finished gasoline and fuel oil to the regional distributors and local retailers. Soon, fuel oil tanks were showing up in every little town alongside the coal dealer's unloading trestle.

The geography of the business spread out, as oilfields in Texas and the Southwest eclipsed Pennsylvania in production, and refineries sprang up all across the country to provide the gasoline and fuel oil that was growing in popularity as the automobile made its mark on the twentieth century. Many of the refineries were located on

products from textiles to structural, building, and packaging materials with a wide variety of strength, texture, and flexibility. The chemical components for making plastic, like propylene, would be derived from petroleum in a refinery and shipped to another plant to be processed into a specific form of raw plastic. The final products, however, could be molded and fabricated in an infinite number of small factories scattered throughout the country.

Plastic is formed into its end product by a careful application of heat and pressure in processes ranging from injection molding to extrusion to vacuum forming. A small company with an injection molding machine and a good pattern-maker could go into the plastic-product manufacturing business. And the railroad was usually the best way to receive his raw plastic from the chemical plant. The most common form of distribution involved plastic pellets that could be handled like a

Tank car trains were America's lifeline during World War II. Oil that normally would have been carried by coastal tankers was diverted inland to the rails when Nazi and Japanese submarines prowled the oceans just off the North American coasts. Here an oil-burning Santa Fe 2-8-0 is gathering up oil tank cars of various sizes. The smaller cars carried the heavier liquids. RAILFAN & RAILROAD *COLLECTION*

Carrying Water to the Ocean

WATER TRAIN AT PIGEON KEY

It was Henry M. Flagler's Florida East Coast Railway that opened up the entire state of Florida to become the winter and retirement refuge that we know today. His railroad reached Miami from the north in 1896, but Flagler saw great potential in the seaport of Key West, which is closer to Cuba than it is to the U.S. mainland. Passenger and freight traffic to Havana and the Panama Canal prompted him to build "the railroad that went to sea" over more than 100 miles of islands that link Key West to the tip of mainland Florida. In 1906 the Key West Extension began skipping from island to island with long bridges over the open sea and reached the city of Key West on January 22, 1912.

The Florida Keys had one serious drawback, however. Surrounded by the ocean, they were too small and shallow to develop natural underground tables of fresh water; wells on the Keys would bring up salt water. In the sailing-ship days, rainwater was collected in cisterns for drinking water, or fresh water was brought in by ships. During construction of the railroad, water was hauled in huge oaken casks on flatcars.

By the 1920s, small communities with water towers sprang up along the railroad, and they were served by the continuing operation of water trains. About that time, the FEC began using petroleum-style tank cars converted to water service and pulled them with 4-8-2 steam locomotives.

Tiny Pigeon Key, at milepost 48, was the first construction camp between Marathon and Key West, and it was vital to the building of the Seven Mile Bridge between Marathon and Little Duck Key. Although it has been populated since 1910, Pigeon Key is so small and low that the railroad never touched the soil but soared overhead on a high trestle. All of its fresh water and most supplies were brought in by rail to the water tower and depot, high alongside the bridge. The above artwork, entitled "Water Train at Pigeon Key," by John Roberts of Big Pine Key, depicts 4-8-2 No. 431 pausing there to discharge water around 1933.

The Great Hurricane of 1935 destroyed the line at Matecumbe, about 30 miles north of Marathon, and the railroad was never reopened. Many of the railroad bridges were utilized in the creation of the Overseas Highway in 1938, and water was then trucked in to those few still living in the Middle Keys. The Aqueduct Pipeline was opened in 1949, primarily to serve the expanding operations of the U.S. Navy at Key West. Then and now, the water was tapped from the well-fields in Florida City on the mainland. Pigeon Key looks very much like this today, with the railroad bridge converted to a roadway and the island maintained as an historic site.

"dry liquid" in pipes or conveyors and simply loaded into the hopper bins of the molding machines to be melted and shaped. The 100-ton covered hopper was the perfect vehicle for transporting the pellets from the chemical plant to the manufacturer. With any luck at all, the finished product could also be shipped out in boxcars.

MODERN TANK CARS

Following World War II, the petrochemical industry expanded rapidly as new products and manufacturing techniques produced all sorts of commodities that could be carried in tank cars. As a result, four general characteristics developed for tank cars: pressurized or non-pressurized and insulated or non-insulated. A car could be built with a combination of two of the four, i.e., non-insulated and non-pressurized or insulated and pressurized.

A non-pressurized car would have an expansion dome on top and a discharge valve on the bottom, while a pressurized car (which was designed to carry loads at an internal pressure of 100 to 500 p.s.i.) would have a covered manhole on top instead of a dome and no bottom valve. For safety, all loading and unloading of a pressurized car is done from the top. A non-insulated car would have its steel shell exposed on the outside, while an insulated car would have a thin steel jacket covering the insulating material around the inner tank.

The earlier tank cars were limited by the capacity of their trucks (wheel assemblies), which could carry only 30 to 40 tons. These cars were usually less than 30 feet long and carried a 6,000–8,000-gallon payload. By the 1940s, however, the 50-ton truck was standard, and the tank car grew to 40 feet and up to 12,000 gallons. The size

Although there are strict limits on the size and capacities of tank cars, particularly regarding potentially hazardous or explosive cargoes, some truly impressive cars are used to carry relatively lightweight and benign materials like this vinyl chloride tanker riding on span-bolster trucks at Waller, Texas, on December 8, 1984. The lack of any outlet pipes on the bottom of the tank indicates that this is a pressurized car. TOM KLINE

Sussex County, New Jersey, purchased about 20 miles of the abandoned Lehigh & Hudson River Railroad below Warwick, New York, to maintain service to the Eastern Propane distribution facility at Sparta Junction, and the New York, Susquehanna & Western was contracted to operate it. In the spring of 1986, an NYS&W Alco road-switcher trundles southward through Baird's Farm just below Warwick with two propane loads for Eastern.

of a car was not necessarily directly proportional to its capacity, however, for the loads could very widely in density and weight. Gaseous liquid cars could be very large, while a car for a thick lubricant would have to be relatively small for the same weight.

By 1960, the 100-ton truck was available, and most track had been upgraded to handle heavier locomotives and cars, and the tank car suddenly grew impressively in size. The biggest cars today are 23,500 gallons for non-pressurized and 33,500 gallons for pressurized. After some disastrous accidents and resulting explosions and fires in the 1960s, the Department of Transportation limited the overall capacity of tank cars and mandated safety elements such as end shields and "shelf" couplers that would stay locked together in case of a derailment.

Not all tank cars carry chemicals relating to the plastic industry, however. Gasoline and fuel oil and propane are common consumer fuels that are widely transported by rail. Caustic soda and acid used in a variety of manufacturing processes need to be moved, as well. Agricultural chemicals like ammonia fertilizer help farmers grow the crops

that often end up in tank cars, like corn syrup and vegetable oils. The customers and railroads keep careful records of each car and the loads that it has carried to avoid contamination.

Compared to highway transportation, where every private automobile on the road is a potential cause for an accident with a truck, the rails are by far the safest way to transport hazardous liquids and pressurized gasses overland. While the mishaps can be spectacular and make horrifying headlines, the safety record of the railroads is superb, and the durability and "wreck-proofing" of tank cars is being continuously improved with new manufacturing techniques and design innovations.

Rail transportation gives the petrochemical industry a flexibility that cannot be matched by other modes of liquid transport. Supplies of crude oil or refined products can change rapidly with market conditions, and railroad cars can go immediately where they are needed, unlike a pipeline, for instance, that has a severely fixed route. While motor trucks are ideal for local distribution of small loads, only the rails have the capacity and flexibility to keep the industry working efficiently.

Coal and oil are formed by the same geological processes and are often found in the ground in close proximity to each other. Such is the case with the coalfield and oil patch near Craig, Colorado, which is served by the legendary Denver & Salt Lake line that became the Craig Branch of the Denver & Rio Grande Western. Here at Orestod Junction, just east of Bond, Colorado, on July 26, 1977, a three-way meet is underway as eastbound coal train 742 out of Craig waits on the branch while westbound 741 pulls up the main line to get out of the way. Meanwhile Salt Lake City–Denver merchandiser 148 was holding on the eastbound main for 741 to clear the single-track line to Denver. When 741 got past the branch switch and stopped, the merchandiser departed for Denver with coal train 742 off the branch right behind him. With the two eastbounds out of the way, 741 backed up to the switch and headed west up the branch, carrying empty tank cars for oil loading among a few other cars for customers on the branch. It was all in a day's work of moving freight through the Colorado Rockies.

The Amador Central is a 12-mile short line in the Mother Lode region of California southeast of Sacramento that survives on the American Forest Products lumber mill at Martell. One of the Amador Central's two Baldwin S12 switchers has a train of boxcars of lumber and bulkhead flats carrying bundles of particle board bound for interchange at Ione (originally named "Bedbug") and the Southern Pacific branch out of Galt. At the time of this 1993 photo, the Amador Central was making about two trips a week.

10

Out of the
Woods

Timber is America's renewable resource. It can be harvested and replanted and harvested again. It's just that the cycle is usually calculated in terms of decades, rather than months or years. As Americans pioneered their way westward, they literally hacked their way along, turning the virgin forests into homes and fireplace fuel. By the twentieth century, however, conservation and "tree farming" became recognized as good business, and

Pulpwood is used in making paper, and it is shipped in standard lengths on special bulkhead flatcars known as "pulpwood racks." Throughout the country, from the Deep South to Upper Michigan and the Pacific Northwest, pulpwood is gathered from small "loadouts" that require little more than a siding and a special forklift end loader. Here on the Georgia Railroad "Cheese Job" local out of Atlanta, a brakeman was swinging off a pulpwood rack that was being picked up from a siding in June 1971. MIKE SCHAFER

although some brutal pillaging of the landscape continued, most of the larger companies saw that their future would be guaranteed only by careful management and responsible harvesting.

Trees are by their very nature big and heavy, and railroads soon found a vital place in the logging industry. Since wood floats, natural waterways were used extensively in logging operations, getting the trees from the woods to the sawmills.

By the late 1800s, steam power was making its way into the woods with steam-driven log skidders that used chains and cables to move logs from the cutting sites to creek basins and railheads. Huge and efficient sawmills were driven by steam power.

Because a logging operation moves through the woods as trees are harvested and new stands are marked for cutting, the railway track tended to

The West Virginia Pulp & Paper sawmill at Cass, West Virginia, shut down in 1960, but its mountain-climbing railroad became the historic Cass Scenic Railroad. Shay No. 2 poses beside the mill in May 1978.

be temporary and makeshift. Conventional locomotives did not fare well on such trackwork, and in 1873 a Michigan logger, Ephriam Shay, devised a clever gear-driven steam locomotive that used four-wheel trucks like those of a freight car to negotiate the uncertain track. A horizontal shaft connected gears on the wheels to a set of cylinders mounted on the locomotive frame. Flexible couplings permitted the trucks to twist and turn freely while still transmitting the full power to the wheels. The "Shay" locomotive and its imitators, the Climax and Heisler, became the universal power for deep-woods logging operations everywhere. Ephriam Shay had his subsequent locomotives built by the Lima Machine Works in Ohio (a manufacturer of sawmill machinery), and within a few years Lima became one of the "Big Three" American steam locomotive builders. The Shays were very powerful but slow, with a maximum speed of about 12 MPH, but they were extremely flexible and could dig in and climb unbelievably steep grades.

Logging railroads spread throughout North America in the late nineteenth and early twentieth centuries. They were generally broken down into two types: woods lines and road hauls. The woods lines were characterized by light, temporary track reaching directly to the cutting sites, while the road hauls would tend to be more substantial and permanent railroads from central reloads to the sawmills. Geared engines were the typical power on the woods lines, while conventional rod engines could make better speed over the road hauls.

Flatcars were the obvious carriers for logs, with side stakes to keep the "long wood" in line. Some interesting variations were the "skeleton" cars with big U-shaped brackets over the trucks and only a minimal underframe between them, and the "disconnect" cars that consisted of a single independent truck under each end of the load, using the logs themselves as the car frame. These deep-woods logging operations persisted with steam power until after World War II, when heavy motor trucks, bulldozers, and tractors became available to work directly on the ground without the need to lay track.

Although by the new millennium, few deep-woods logging railroads remained, some of the road-hauls survive with modern cars to carry the long wood out to sawmills, and much of the finished lumber still goes out by rail. Nearly every stick of lumber that shows up in a home or building

Logging has always been a "heavy industry," and it was quick to adopt steam power in the nineteenth century. Here in 1984, a steam crane was demonstrating log loading on the Cass Scenic Railroad in West Virginia. The crane has small wheels that ride rails on the log cars to be able to move from car to car for loading.

The Valley & Siletz Railroad makes a road haul of raw logs from the cutting site in the woods to the sawmill in this scene from circa 1950. The 40-mile railroad connected with the Southern Pacific at Independence, Oregon. Note the deluxe crew's seat on the tender! JAMES W. RAVELLI, RAILFAN & RAILROAD COLLECTION

The Graham County Railroad:
1500 miles from Point A to Point A

In 1925, the Bemis Lumber Company completed an 11-mile line-haul railroad from the Southern Railway's Murphy branch at Topton, North Carolina, to its new hardwood sawmill at Robbinsville. The Graham County Railroad continued to operate a pair of Shay geared steam locomotives into the early 1970s when the railroad bought a General Electric 70-ton diesel and continued to serve Robbinsville.

There were only two customers there still shipping by rail: the big hardwood lumber mill and a smaller furniture factory. In the Appalachian spirit of the Hatfields vs. McCoys, however, over the years a feud had developed between the lumber company and the furniture plant. The furniture people refused to buy lumber from the Bemis sawmill.

One day the Southern Railway telephoned the railroad and asked if the Graham County could handle the weight of a chain flatcar loaded with high grade hardwood for the furniture plant. General Manager Dan Ranger replied that they could, and the Southern set the car out at the Topton interchange a few days later. When the paperwork came through on the car, Dan recognized the number, which as he recalled was unusual because it was "all ones and zeros." He checked the books and discovered that the same car had been shipped from Bemis about two weeks earlier!

This load of hardwood had originated at the Bemis mill in Robbinsville and was dispatched in the hands of a broker on a "furtherance" routing to a remote destination—with the intention that

The Graham County's GE has two boxcars and two loads of woodchips bound for the Southern Railway interchange at Topton in April 1974. JIM BOYD

the car would never actually be delivered to that destination. A broker buys and sells commodities—lumber being one of the most common—but never wants the car to actually show up at his own doorstep. The broker thus puts the car on a circuitous routing so that it will be kept moving while he negotiates a sale of the rolling commodity. As soon as the load is sold, it is "rerouted" to the new final customer. An amazing number of freight cars moving across America, including perishable goods, are on such routings, headed for a destination they are never intended to reach.

This particular load had been shipped from Bemis in Robbinsville and was sold through two or three intermediate brokers before it got into the hands of one who was looking for a car of hardwood for the furniture plant. The broker had no idea where the loaded car had originated, but he knew that it met the customer's requirements. Thus, he bought the load, had it forwarded to the furniture plant, and collected his commission.

That chain flat, it turns out, traveled roughly 1,500 miles and was handled by a half dozen different railroads (each of whom got a percentage of the transportation charges) before it was delivered to its final destination—within sight of where it had originated two weeks earlier! The customer never saw the complete paperwork history on the car, and the railroad never hinted that it knew where that carload of lovely wood had come from. But the Graham County collected both origination and termination fees on that particular car. Nice work, if you can get it.

or on the sales floor of Home Depot made part of its journey from the sawmill to the customer by rail. Building materials, in all their various forms, are a very large part of the railroad traffic carried today.

Lumber used to be a traditional boxcar load and still is, but newer packaging and marketing methods make extensive use of special flatcars that can be easily loaded and unloaded with mobile forklift trucks. Bulkhead flatcars have heavy "bookends" to keep the loads from shifting longitudinally in transit, and "centerbeam" cars add a lengthwise middle divider to the end bulkheads to stabilize and secure loads. A center-beam will hold stacks of finished lumber or bundles of standard 4 x 8 sheets of plywood or wallboard that are wrapped in protective paper or plastic in sizes that can be easily handled by a forklift.

PULPWOOD AND PAPER

Not all logging is done to produce lumber. The computer, which was supposed to create the paperless society, has had the effect of generating an even greater demand for paper. Everything from high-grade print stock to newsprint to toilet paper is made from processed wood. Since the wood is ground into pulp in a paper mill and treated with chemicals to utilize its natural fibers, there is no need to ship pulpwood as large logs. In fact, much paper-making wood is shipped in the form of woodchips that are the chopped-up small limbs and trimmings from lumbering operations and sawmills. Wood chips are relatively light in weight and are often shipped in modified high-capacity boxcars or jumbo hoppers. Wood chips are a highly valuable resource, however, and they are often exported by the shipload to paper mills overseas.

In addition to wood chips, paper mills use pulpwood logs that are often harvested in small local patches and trucked to a simple loading siding

The big Pickering Lumber Company sawmill at Standard, California, is served by the Sierra Railroad. A pair of Baldwin S12s is working in front of the chip-loading facility in April 1990, preparing to take carloads of woodchips and finished lumber down to the Southern Pacific interchange at Oakdale. This mill was also the destination of the steam-powered mixed train shown on page 20 at the beginning of Chapter 2.

Kaolin is a fine white clay used as coating material in the production of paper and also porcelain. The powdery nature of kaolin is graphically portrayed in this view of a Sandersville Railroad kaolin-laden train making its way through the undulating Georgia countryside in 1968.

Since the 1960s, chips have become a popular form for transporting wood used in paper mills. Relatively "airy" and lightweight, the chips are usually carried in high-capacity hoppers or converted open-top boxcars. In August 1971 on Canadian Pacific's spectacular Kettle Valley line in southern British Columbia, Fairbanks-Morse diesels have a chip train rolling west of Nelson. MIKE SCHAFER

for rail transport. These are smaller logs that are not suitable for use as building materials, and they are cut to a standard length (usually about five feet) and loaded crosswise in special bulk-head flatcars called "pulpwood racks." These cars typically have a shallow "V" taper lengthwise on their floor to keep the ends of the logs pointed slightly upward to prevent them from shifting off the open sides of the cars.

Pulpwood loading can be found all across the country, but it is particularly common in the Deep South, in the Pacific Northwest, and in the Great Lakes states. A local wag in Texarkana once observed of the yellow-colored pulpwood, "... them 'Arkansas bananas' are the perfect traffic for the Kansas City Southern, since you can't hurt 'em, they won't spoil, and nobody cares when they get there!"

ABOVE: *There seemed to be small pulpwood yards all over the Georgia Railroad in August 1968. The heavyweight combine carried passengers and served as the conductor's office on the Washington–Barnett mixed train. These pulpwood racks have no center beams, but the logs are stacked in two rows on the floor that has a gentle "V" shape toward the center to keep the load from shifting. The cars are loaded and unloaded with forklifts with claws that grasp "handfuls" of logs.*

LEFT: *Modern center-beam flatcars were designed to carry pallets of 4 x 8-foot sheets of 4 x 8 plywood and other lumber that is packaged to protect it from the weather. Here at Archbald, Pennsylvania, in August 2000, shortline Delaware-Lackawanna serves this rudimentary lumber distributor along the Delaware & Hudson main line. The forklift hiding in the shadows at left is the only machine needed to transload lumber from the rail cars to trucks for delivery to nearby lumber yards.*

On the other hand, a Cotton Belt (St. Louis-Southwestern Railroad) crew working into Texarkana tells of the day they had a pulpwood load shift approaching the Ouichata River bridge at Camden, Arkansas. "We were making about 50 MPH when the pulpwood, which had shifted over the side of the car, hit the angled ends of the truss bridge and was propelled straight up into the air. Those logs came raining down on the caboose like cannonshells, making a terrible racket and denting the roof and bashing out every window in the cupola!" Fortunately, the alert crew saw it coming and hit the floor, avoiding any injury. There are now photoelectric beam wide-load detectors protecting all the through-truss bridges on the Cotton Belt.

One of the most famous locations in railroading is Tehachapi Loop between Bakersfield and Mojave, California, and one of the most famous cabooses is the Santa Fe's steel design. These timeless buggies were introduced in the steam era and upgraded over the years while maintaining their distinctive profile. Note the cushion underframe holding the coupler on the caboose in the foreground. Two freights were meeting at Waylong Siding in May 1984; note the second caboose on the track in the center.

11

Cabooses:
End of an Era

Silently gliding along behind all those freight cars was the caboose. Born circa 1850, the caboose served as the train's "office" (think of a train as a rolling warehouse, which in essence it is). Here, the train's conductor carried out his paperwork—checking car waybills and detailing the switchlists—and managed the train's operations, sharing space with his able assistants, the brakeman and flagman. In earlier days and on long runs that found the

During the steam era, the caboose was a rolling hotel room and restaurant for railroad crews, who worked together and shared the housekeeping chores. Caboose cooking on the coal stove could range from magnificent to ghastly, depending on the skills of the individual crewmen. Here a brakeman peels the potatoes while the conductor tends to the stove in a New Haven caboose in the early 1950s.
RAILFAN & RAILROAD *COLLECTION*

Oops! There were hazards to being on the rear end of a freight train. It was fairly common to be hit by another train, but it was rather rare for a caboose to strike a structure. In August 1941 at Grand Haven, Michigan, however, a Pere Marquette freight train shoved backward onto a swing bridge that was opening and climbed the end truss. The resulting photo and a clever caption would make a great motivational poster! RAILFAN & RAILROAD *COLLECTION*

crew far from home, the caboose also doubled as a home away from home, complete with bunks, kitchen, and toilet facilities as well as a complement of tools, safety supplies, and spare freight-car parts.

Today, cabooses are a rare sight, having been replaced by the technology of the 1980s in the form of a box with a blinking light that rides in the rear coupler of the last car. You can still see cabooses in some local-freight and work-train services, though.

The story at the rear of the train really started at the front, in the cab of the locomotive. Early steam engines were compact affairs with barely enough room for the fireman and the engineer. Though the layman might think otherwise, the engineer is not in charge of the train. True, he or she runs the locomotive(s), but the train's "boss" is the conductor—the final on-board authority in determining when and where the train moves and what work is to be done. The conductor

coordinates his movements with dispatchers, yardmasters, and even local station agents and the customers themselves. In steam days he had as many as three brakemen and a flagman to help him move the train over the road and handle the switching.

All this help needed a place to ride. The earliest trains usually had a combination of freight and passenger cars, and the crew would simply ride in a coach or baggage car. As more and more freight-only trains developed, however, the need for a "conductor's car" became obvious. It wasn't long before a boxcar was commandeered to serve as a place for the conductor and company to take refuge from the weather. Its place at the rear of the train was mandated by the need to have someone back there to protect the train from rear-end collisions (in unsignaled territory, the flagman was required to walk back a safe distance whenever the train would stop, to warn an approaching train that the track ahead was occupied) and to throw switches behind the train whenever it entered a siding. With the advent of air brakes, it was also handy to have someone on the rear end to signal the engineer when the brakes were operating properly.

In the early days, railroad management saw little reason to worry about the safety and well-being of crew members—after all, there was an inexhaustible supply of individuals who needed jobs, and this new car was definitely an additional expense, not a revenue-maker. But at some point in the 1840s, the little red caboose appeared, and like most inventions born of necessity, it led a long life.

Like the tradition of the stagecoaches and freight wagons that preceded it, railroading was considered an outside job, but with the power of a locomotive, weight was less of a problem on a train than on a wagon, and enclosed locomotive cabs and cozy cabooses soon appeared. The first cabooses were simply modified boxcars with windows, a stove, and a side door with ladder steps. Before long, the walls by the doors had pegs for coats, and the top of the stove had a simmering pot of coffee. The toolbox lid had a cushion laid on it for a seat or a bed. As paperwork was added to document the movement of cars, an ambitious conductor probably adapted a desk to hold his waybills and train orders.

The classic caboose was developed in the 1860s as a combination of features of a boxcar and a passenger car, along with a few unique innovations like the rooftop "cupola." With its high-mounted seats and windows looking out over the roof, the cupola permitted the crewmen to watch the train as it negotiated curves. In areas where there was double track, when opposing trains passed, the crew of one train would inspect the condition of the other as it rolled by. The "highball" signal given by a crew member from one caboose to another meant that everything looked okay.

The caboose was built more like a boxcar than a coach, with simple, solid sides penetrated by just a few windows. The boxcar-style side door with sharply vertical steps was difficult to get into and out of when the train was moving, so the end platform, with overhanging roof and conveniently angled "Pullman" steps, was borrowed from passenger-car technology. (A few of the side-door cabooses survived well into the 1940s, however, and with their blunt, platformless ends, they were often referred to as "mulie end" cabooses.)

The end platforms gave the crew members a safe place to stand outside to inspect other trains and to view the railroad itself. Some railroads, particularly in the East, considered it valuable to have the platform extend the full width to the edge of the car so that the crewman could safely look both forward and back along the side. These cabooses used cast metal "tender steps" like those

Cabooses were an unwanted but necessary expense in the days of five-man crews before radio communication, and many railroads built their own inexpensive cabooses by converting boxcars or building new carbodies atop locomotive tender underframes. Here in Augusta, Georgia, in 1968 was a Georgia Railroad caboose that was obviously created from an outside-braced wooden boxcar with steel ends.

RIGHT: The American rail labor union movement has its beginning in this Delaware & Hudson Canal Company caboose at Oneonta, New York, on September 13, 1883, when railroaders gathered to form what became the Brotherhood of Railroad Trainmen. This typical four-wheel "bobber" of the era is now displayed under shelter in Oneonta. JIM SHAUGHNESSY

BELOW: The "Northeastern" caboose was designed by the USRA during World War I but never built. In 1924, the Reading adopted an all-steel version of the USRA design, and it soon spread to Reading's neighbors like the Lehigh Valley, Jersey Central, and Western Maryland. Many found their way to other parts of the country, however, like this ex-Reading car on the Ashley, Drew & Northern at Crossett, Arkansas, in 1968. Note the "tender style" vertical steps on the platforms, compared to the more common "Pullman steps" shown on all the other cabooses in this chapter.

between a locomotive and tender rather than the deeply angled Pullman steps. Modern cabooses, like those on the Illinois Central, had the best elements of both types, with longer end platforms with side-protected full-width portions as well as Pullman steps.

In the era before airbrakes, the brakeman's job was quite hazardous. In fact, the issue of safety spawned the Brotherhood of Railroad Trainmen—in a caboose on the Delaware & Hudson Canal Company in 1883. Railroad management of that era had little care for the safety of the working man. That little caboose was about the only comfort that a brakeman's job afforded, and the pros and cons of a trainman's union must have been argued about in many a caboose all over America.

By the 1920s, cabooses had gone from being homemade shacks on wheels to looking like wooden versions of the last cabooses built in the 1970s. Even railroads that continued to build their own equipment used standardized parts and dimensions in order to use commercially available hardware. In time, cabooses were built with a conductor's desk, storage lockers, an icebox, beds, and a straight-to-the-ballast toilet, in addition to the

familiar coal or oil stove. The underframes of the cars were originally made of wood, just like the carbody itself. As train tonnage increased and along with it the power of pusher locomotives—which helped shove trains from behind up steep mountain grades—the wooden frame under the caboose became the weak link. After many accidents crushed cabooses, steel frames became the industry standard. In time, the carbody itself would be fabricated entirely of steel, as well.

As freight cars grew larger and taller, the cupola became less effective, as a single high car could block most of the over-the-top view. Some railroads tried side bay windows instead of a cupola,

and the idea caught on. With its seats high above the floor, the cupola was always a potential safety hazard in a car that was subject to the severe slack action of a mile-long train. The bay-window design avoided this potential chance of falling. Wood and steel bay-window cabooses achieved popularity in the 1940s. They were cheaper to build than a cupola caboose and were safer to work in. Some railroads still preferred the cupola, however, and in the 1960s the caboose-builders picked up the old idea of the cupola that stuck out from the side like a bay window but retained its location on the roof. These "extended-vision" cupolas were essentially high-mounted bay windows and were particularly

The interior of this Illinois Central 1960s-era steel caboose shows the cushioned benches that served as overnight bunks, as well as the coal stove and water basin. An open-chute toilet was in the closed compartment on the left, just beyond the cupola. Note the overhead safety grab-iron running the length of the car beneath the peak of the roof. Surprisingly, into the late 1960s, Iowa Division crews out of Freeport, Illinois, would sleep in their caboose during their layover in downtown Chicago. ILLINOIS CENTRAL, RAILFAN & RAILROAD *COLLECTION*

As freight cars grew taller in the diesel era, the cupola often became useless for viewing the train if a high car was coupled ahead of it. In the 1950s the railroads began to experiment with bay-window cabooses. The floor-level bays were also much safer than the cupolas, where a sudden lurch from slack action made the elevated seats a potential hazard for falling. The idea of the bay window caught on, and they found wide acceptance. In July 1968 this former-Nickel Plate caboose was bound for Peoria on the old Nickel Plate's Lake Erie & Western line, banging across the Gilman–St. Louis line of the Illinois Central at Gibson City, Illinois. The Nickel Plate cabooses were unusual in having the small side windows near the roof for the overhead bunks inside.

popular with Western railroads that had generous lineside clearances.

Electricity came to the caboose in the 1950s, with axle-driven alternators that generated 115 volts AC and could charge storage batteries. This led to water coolers and electric refrigeration and heat. The electric power also help popularize train radios, which, ironically, set the scene for the demise of the caboose.

The radio revolution started with a heavy box about the size of a personal computer, that was full of vacuum tubes and transformers and had to be bolted to a shelf. Using a telephone handset, it was an improvement over lanterns and flags, but it was too heavy to carry around and not immune to the shocks and jolts that typify the ride of a long freight train. Early radios needed a locomotive or caboose as a source of power, so they were not a threat to crew sizes nor the caboose itself. All switching still had to be done line-of-sight with hand signals. Even with no handbrakes to set, a switch crew still needed two or three men just to "pass signals" around curves. Today, the transistorized radio fits into a railroader's jacket pocket and weighs about as much as a can of Pepsi.

By the 1970s, caboose design had become down right cushy. All manner of safety equipment was installed including high-back seats and seat belts. Sharp edges on furniture and fixtures were eliminated in an effort to reduce injuries from sudden stops. Cushioned underframes, widely used by that time to keep freight from being damaged from the shock of starting or stopping trains, were adapted to cabooses to protect crews from those same shocks. All these improvements cost money, though, and by the mid-1980s the price of a new caboose had reached $80,000. It was claimed that if all the cabooses in service at that time were replaced, the cost would be over a billion dollars. The cost of operating and maintaining cabooses on the Burlington Northern in 1982 was figured at $36,000 each, and they operated 1,120 of them.

Technology caught up with the caboose in the form of the "End Of Train" Device (EOT or ETD). Although that term was used by the industry, train crews came up with a much easier-to-remember one: FRED, for "Flashing Rear-End Device"—the marriage of improved air-brake technology and the radio. The best ones, called "smart FREDs," have telemetry equipment that can radio information to the engineer: what the air-line pressure is; if there has been a significant change in air-line pressure; which way the end of the train is rolling; and if the rear signal light is working. These are the battery-powered "black boxes" with the blinking red light that you see on the ends of freight trains these days. Ironically, it is the standard vertical hole in the knuckle—left over from the link-and-pin days—that is used to mount most FREDs

ILLINOIS CENTRAL   9677

In the early 1960s, the Illinois Central took all the best elements of caboose technology and combined them in this new design, built in the company's Centralia (Illinois) Car Shop. The "extended vision" cupola combined the advantages of both the cupola and bay window, and the long end platforms provided a safe place to stand while looking around the side of the car while still using the recessed Pullman steps. (The advantage of the "tender steps" on the Northeastern caboose is that the full-width platform permitted a crewman to look around the car to inspect the train or to catch train orders handed up "on the fly" from the ground.) These fine cars had cushioned underframes, electric lighting, and oil-fired stoves. The 9677 was at Chicago's Markham Yard in 1970.

today. A "dumb FRED" can be anything from a blinking light to a simple red flag stuck in the last knuckle.

Born on the Florida East Coast Railway as a high-tech union buster, the FRED and the portable trainman's radio led to the elimination of the full-crew laws on America's railroads. Until that time, Class 1 railroads ran trains with three to five crewmembers, depending on the type of train, mileage, and distance traveled. The success of the original FREDs on the Florida East Coast set the stage for the union showdowns of the 1980s. The FEC eliminated cabooses in 1972 and moved their occupants to locomotive cabs. All of this was instrumental in providing the rest of America's railroads with the mandate to follow suit. By 1982, the two-man crew of today had become the industry standard.

Interestingly, the caboose is still with us today in spirit, and it is highly visible if you know where to look. With the airbrake and radio eliminating the need for the brakeman on road freights, the two-man crew consists of the engineer and the conductor, while locals that need to do switching

In the years before portable radios, a freight train needed a five-man crew to pass hand signals for line-of-sight work. Here in 1990, the author demonstrates the circular "back 'em up" night signal with a hand lantern. Hand signals were often different between daytime and night. The caboose was needed to carry and house large crews. MIKE DEL VECCHIO

Railroading had a more human face in the steam era, and the "little red caboose" was the perfect punctuation mark for the end of the train. In October 1955, Colorado & Southern's Denver–Billings freight No. 77 is passing through Fort Collins, Colorado, with a caboose "double-hinder." The white-shirted operator has just "hooped up" train orders to the brakeman and is holding the empty fork that had delivered the same orders to the locomotive crew. Did the boys on the bicycles realize that this train was symbolically carrying the kerosene marker lamps, marking not only the end of a train, but of an entire era? WALTER L. McMURTRY, RAILFAN & RAILROAD COLLECTION

en route may get a brakeman to speed up the work. They all ride in the cab of the locomotive, and the new units have bigger "super cabs" that include a desk for the conductor and often even have a radio-linked computer that can print out everything from train orders and clearance forms to switchlists and customer car requests.

So the little red (or yellow, or blue, or orange) caboose behind the train is now right up front with high cheekbones beneath the windshield and the triad of headlight and ditch lights that make a modern freight train so distinctive as it approaches.

The freight train may look very different today from the 1830s concept of the Stephensons of England and the fledgling Baltimore & Ohio, but the tracks have the same gauge between the rails and the same economic purpose behind them. Those trains are the very lifeblood of the continent on the move. They were created by private money, and they paid their taxes and rewarded their investors—and along the way they built a nation out of a wilderness.

Not a bad day's work.

This is FRED. "He" has replaced the caboose with technology. FRED stands for "Flashing Rear-End Device," and it has combined with the use of radios to reduce train crews from five people to two. This "smart FRED" on a Delaware-Lackawanna grain train at Scranton, Pennsylvania, in 2000, constantly radios to the engineer data on airbrake trainline pressure, whether or not the car is moving, and in which direction it is moving. Note the hose that attaches to the airbrake hose. The FRED is locked onto the coupler and is light enough to be lifted by one person.

Although a few cabooses remain for special service, often involving extensive switching or long back-up moves, they have become just another piece of vanishing Americana. On April 29, 2000, this beautifully restored Wabash "streamlined cupola" caboose was on a special photo freight at the Monticello Railway Museum in Illinois. STEVE BARRY

Index